THE LAKE MINNETONKA GUIDE TO
SHORELINE GARDENS

CREATED & PUBLISHED
BY:

URBAN ECOSYSTEMS
THE NATURE OF CITIES

WWW.URBANECOSYSTEMSINC.COM
MINNEAPOLIS, MN

Funding provided by the Minnehaha Creek Watershed District

MINNEHAHA CREEK
WATERSHED DISTRICT

TABLE OF CONTENTS

INTRODUCTION

MINNESOTA LOVES ITS LAKES.

Lakes are an iconic part of the Minnesota landscape and an essential component of our region's ecological and cultural identity. For untold generations, people have settled beside the water. Not only because of its value as a resource, but also because of its serenity and beauty. Being near the water inspires a sense of connectedness with nature and the many living creatures with whom we share the planet. Minnesota's lakes are part of the rich natural heritage that sustains our communities and attracts thousands of visitors annually. People come to swim, boat, and fish, but also to enjoy the scenery, relax with friends and family, and to observe the wildlife. Owning a house on the lake, be it a rustic cabin or a large estate, is a dream for many Americans.

If Minnesota is the Land of 10,000 Lakes, then Lake Minnetonka is emblematic of how its people choose to live and recreate on the water. As the largest lake in the Twin Cities metropolitan area, Lake Minnetonka has been a major destination since the late 1800s. Urbanites flocked to its lakeshore hotels and resorts and began building lakefront homes as retreats from urban life. A streetcar line once connected the town of Excelsior to Minneapolis, and a fleet of commuter boats carried people to destinations around the lake. During the 20th century, the shoreline around the lake developed into a patchwork of upscale communities that have acquired a fashionable and exclusive image, making the lake a trend setter in the region. It has a large and diverse fish population that attracts anglers from around the country and is a regional hotspot for boating and lake culture.

Given its size and character, Lake Minnetonka brings into focus two ways of understanding lakes and our relationship to them. The first is to view lakes as places, a public commons, each with its own customs and values. The second way is to view lakes as an ecosystem, an invisible cycle that transfers energy and nutrients to support the plant and animal communities of the lake. These two modes of viewing provide us with a lens to approach how we design and manage our landscapes. Private landowners have very little direct control over the open water, but their collective actions on their own land have a significant impact.

We value lakes
as recreational spaces and real estate amenities.

Lakefront property owners pay a premium for the privilege of living on the water. According to the real estate website Zillow.com, waterfront properties are typically worth double the value of comparable non-waterfront homes in their vicinity. Key features that people look for include boat access, views, level sites, privacy, and proximity to water. Given these priorities, we have altered the landscape to suit our preferences in ways that have had dramatic impacts on the lake ecosystem.

We build houses and driveways near the water and direct the added runoff into the lake. We value the expansive views across the water and so we remove the trees and shrubs along the water's edge. People want access to the water and generally don't enjoy wading through the tall grass, muck, and aquatic vegetation so we often clear this vegetation away. Once it has been replaced with a large green lawn or sandy beach it no longer is able to prevent erosion along the shoreline and often must be stabilized with boulder rip-rap armoring. People want their property to look nice from the water, so they frame their home with landscaping that suits their aesthetic preferences and exudes the image they seek to project.

Over time these transformations can lead to a tragedy of the commons as the character of our lakes changes both as ecosystems and places. The destruction of habitat leads to fewer interactions with wildlife. Increased pollutant loading from streets, driveways, and over fertilized lawns can lead to algae blooms and degradation in water quality. Likewise, as tree line and shoreline vegetation is cleared around a lake, it can transition from a quiet natural character to one that is more suburban in character. Large expanses of lawn and houses then become the most noticeable features of the water's edge. This conflicts with our other understanding of lakes as natural areas and productive ecosystems.

The place where the land and water meet is of great significance from an ecological perspective.
The lake does not end at the water's edge.

When the last ice age ended and the glaciers retreated from the Minnesota landscape, they left thousands of freshwater lakes and streams in their wake. As vegetation and wildlife returned, these waterbodies became the habitat patches and corridors that enabled species to spread and proliferate across the landscape. Minnesota became the place where the northern coniferous forests, the eastern deciduous forests and the tall grass prairie met, making it a crossroads of biodiversity. The Mississippi Flyway, a massive migration route for waterfowl and shorebirds, is centered around the Mississippi River and the lakes and wetlands of our region. Within this larger context, every lake has its own complex ecology that is shaped by its unique aquatic and terrestrial environment.

By taking a step back we can see that the shoreline and the land around the lake are all part of a large and interconnected ecosystem. Shorelines function as corridors for wildlife to move through the landscape and are brimming with life. They are a nexus of activity for terrestrial and aquatic wildlife. Emergent vegetation provides cover for spawning fish and an ideal feeding ground for waterfowl. Turtles sun themselves on glacial boulders while pollinators such as bees and butterflies draw nectar from the shoreline vegetation. Muskrats graze on the emergent plants while deer and other mammals come to drink the water. Above it all, raptors and songbirds circle overhead.

It is easy to forget that people have long been part of these ecosystems as well. Evidence exists of human settlement in Minnesota as early as 8,000 BCE, with many important archaeological sites located along lakes and rivers. The first peoples of Minnesota settled around the lakes where they hunted, trapped, and foraged. As their cultures evolved, they began to systematically transform the landscape to serve their needs. They transplanted or seeded useful plants into areas where they wanted them to grow. They burned large tracts of forest and prairie land to create ideal hunting conditions, to prepare land for agriculture, and to make the landscape easier to traverse. They managed shoreline landscapes to create habitat for desirable species such as beavers and waterfowl and to cultivate medicinal plants. The Ojibwe and Dakota people were dependent on the wild rice harvest to sustain them through the harsh winters and consider it sacred to their way of life. Their cultural practices responded to the changing of the seasons, the natural productivity of the landscape, and a cultivated sense of place. Through these activities we not only transformed the character of these landscapes but also imbued them with meaning and significance. In this respect, all that has changed since then is our attitude towards the landscape and our capacity to transform it to our own ends.

The simplest action that a shoreline property owner can take to reduce their impact on water quality is to plant resilient vegetation along the shoreline to stabilize the soil and filter upland runoff.

Shorelines can be harsh environments that are challenging to plant. They typically experience flooding, drought, ice heaving, wave action, and human disturbance. Likewise, lakes and wetlands typically have complex government regulations that limit what kinds of land alterations or plantings are allowed. As a result, many property owners mow their lawn right down to the water or ignore the shoreline and let it become wild and feral.

One can view the process of replanting the shoreline in different ways. The first is to view the process as a "restoration" of the shoreline vegetation that was present before the property was developed. This approach, which is advocated for by the Minnesota Department of Natural Resources (DNR), involves identifying native plant communities that exist in similar shoreline conditions and developing a design from that palette. Vegetative buffer strips provide benefits such as soil stabilization against erosion and wave action, filtration of sediment and nutrients carried by stormwater runoff, and the provision of critical habitat for wildlife. Despite these benefits, there are a number of drawbacks to the shoreline restoration approach that limit its appeal to property owners. One major limitation is that native restoration plantings require specialized knowledge to design, establish, and maintain, which limits the ability of many designers and contractors to implement these projects. Without expert horticultural knowledge, property owners are often unable to distinguish between weeds and desirable species. Thus without proper management, the destiny of most restoration plantings is a weedy, disorganized mess.

In this sense, a restoration planting is really just a garden. Then why limit these gardens only to native species when a range of design options exist with more diverse aesthetic qualities, simplified maintenance regimes, and comparable habitat value?

By re-imagining the shoreline as a garden space and buffer strip, design alternatives to turfgrass or native plantings emerge that retain all the benefits of traditional shoreline restorations.

They are managed spaces that have formal qualities, yet at the same time are ever growing and changing. A garden is a dialog with nature, where we direct the natural productivity of plants, soil, and water to create spaces that have purpose and meaning. There is a proverb, "As is the garden, so is the gardener." Gardens are an opportunity to create an environment that is your own place in the world. The challenge arises in landscapes that are difficult to shape and manage.

Lakeshore property owners essentially have two front yards. While the traditional landscape is largely concerned with curb appeal, the shoreline landscape requires more sophistication. Not only must it never harm the lake, it must also handle the challenging conditions at the water's edge and generate shore appeal in a highly visible location. As a result, the shoreline landscape becomes an expression of your relationship to the lake and your community.

This book is intended to serve as a visioning tool to help property owners and landscape professionals understand the range of options that exist when planning a shoreline garden. The content is broken into chapters. *The Shoreline Zone* explores the ecological, spatial, and social context of shorelines and documents many common Minnesota shoreline conditions. *Designing Your Shoreline Garden* provides a set of design principles and guidance for selecting the style and organization of your garden. It then goes on to show example projects and renderings that illustrate a range of shoreline garden design possibilities. *Stabilizing Your Shoreline* identifies techniques which will prevent erosion and improve the resiliency and effectiveness of your shoreline garden. *Regulations and Resources* covers the rules and regulations governing shoreline gardens and the process of navigating them. This chapter also provides information about cost share grant opportunities that can offset the cost of installing a shoreline garden and other technical resources. *Establishing Your Shoreline Garden* covers the process of planting, watering, and maintaining your shoreline garden with additional content regarding proper weed and invasive species control. The last chapter is the *Shoreline Garden Plant Guide*, which contains a selection of excellent plants for shoreline gardens and recommendations for their use.

This book will provide you with the necessary knowledge and inspiration to plant your own shoreline garden between green and blue.

Shorelines come in all shapes and sizes. Each one has been shaped by the hydrology of the lake, but also by the people and wildlife that inhabit it. There is not a one size fits all solution when designing a shoreline garden, but the design process begins by understanding the existing conditions and the site context.

THE SHORELINE ZONE

THE SHORELINE ZONE
an ecological crossroads

In a natural, unaltered condition, the shoreline zone is a hub of biodiversity and ecological activity. Shorelines are places where upland and aquatic ecological communities meet. The specific plant and animal species that exist in these areas are highly dependent on the site context, but are largely determined by the level of moisture that is present in the soil. Certain species require permanent moisture while others will only grow in well drained conditions. To a trained eye, the presence of certain plants becomes an indicator of the relative saturation of the soils. In addition, the water levels of shoreline areas tend to fluctuate. This means that successful shoreline plants must be adapted to a range of moisture conditions. When selecting shoreline plants it is critical to understand this moisture regime as it will determine if plants are able to survive when the water levels change. The rendering below shows the shift from aquatic to upland plant communities for a typical Minnesota shoreline.

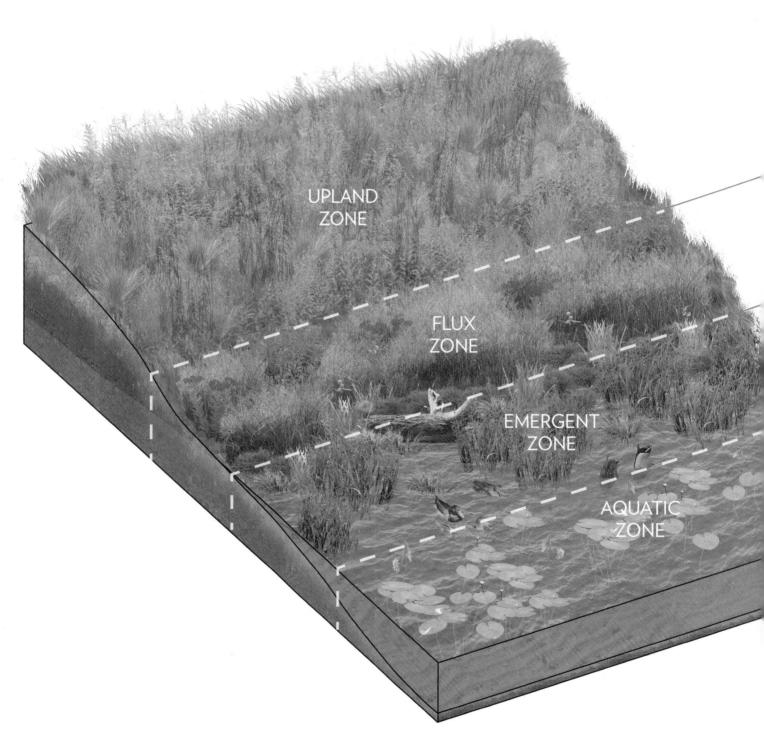

UPLAND ZONE

FLUX ZONE

EMERGENT ZONE

AQUATIC ZONE

This is the area that is never saturated with lake water even during high water events. The plant communities present in this area's roots may be able to draw moisture from deeper in the soil profile, but will generally not survive being flooded with water for any length of time.

The flux zone is the most volatile area of the shoreline. This area is subject to regular saturation for long periods of time, but also can dry out completely. As a result, the plants that thrive in this area tend to be adaptable to a wide variety of moisture regimes.

The emergent zone is the shallow area of the shoreline that remains saturated consistently throughout the growing season. It is so named because typically the vegetation in this area's roots are submerged but the foliage emerges from the water.

The aquatic zone includes the open water areas of the lake as well as the shelf of lake bottom where floating and submergent vegetation can grow. This vegetation is able to root on the lake bottom and the plants exist largely underwater.

THE AVERAGE SHORELINE
a missed opportunity

The typical developed shoreline property is often organized with the goals of maximizing views of the lake and creating a neat and well maintained lawn space down to the water. There often is significant investment in landscape improvements around the house itself, but this rarely extends to the shoreline. Given the challenges of landscaping the water's edge, the shoreline is typically left as a marginal turf space. A large expanse of lawn requires costly inputs such as regular mowing, fertilization, and irrigation. Above all else, a huge lawn has very little identity and is a lost opportunity for creating a distinctive and sophisticated lake shore property.

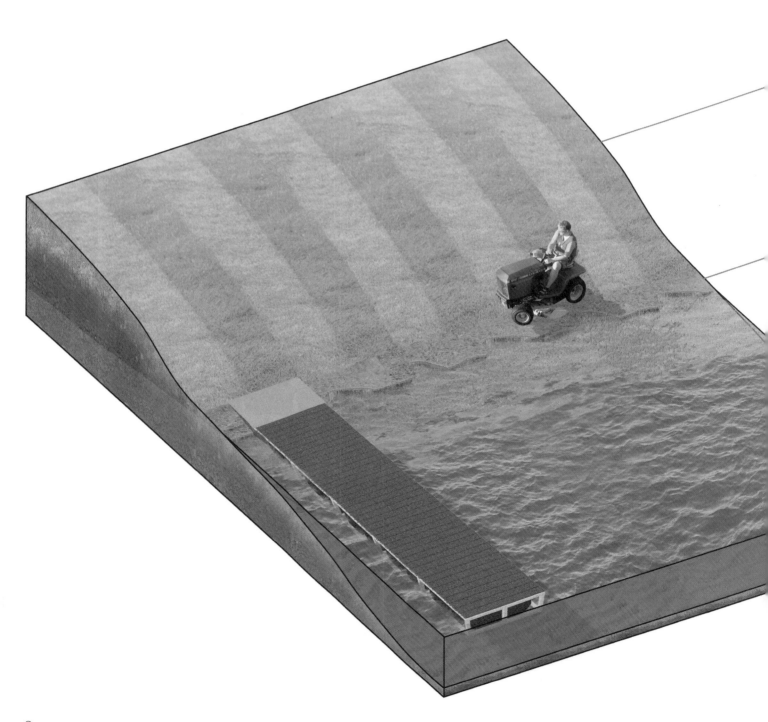

There are a lot of costs to a large expanse of lawn that goes right up to the water's edge. In addition to weekly mowing, fertilization, and irrigation, there are environmental costs as well. Rain storms wash excess fertilizer, leaves, and lawn clippings into the lake. Unless there is a planting along the shore there is no slowing or filtering of these materials. A planting has the added benefit of deterring Canada Geese, who prefer open lawn spaces devoid of potential predators.

A densely vegetated shoreline stabilizes the soil by locking it in place with its roots and dissipating the energy of waves with its leaves and branches. If all of the pre-existing vegetation is removed from the shoreline and replaced with turf grass it no longer has the root structure to stabilize the soil, leading to increased risk of bank collapse.

Nutrients such as phosphorus and nitrogen that are carried to the lake by lawn clippings can lead to algae blooms along shorelines. Algae forms a thick mat across the surface of the water that is unsightly and can be smelly and dangerous for humans and pets. Then in the winter when the algae dies, the decomposition process consumes the dissolved oxygen in the water, threatening fish and other aquatic life.

The added nutrients and sediment that gets washed into the lake ecosystem leads to decreases in water clarity as algae and suspended sediment limit the ability of sunlight to penetrate the water column. If sunlight can no longer reach the lake bottom there is a loss of aquatic vegetation, leading to further loss of dissolved oxygen and destabilization of the aquatic ecosystem.

COMMON SHORELINE CONDITIONS
understanding your shoreline

The natural history of a lake is usually the strongest determinant of its shoreline conditions. This largely relates to the glacial history of the lake. Some lakes are shallow potholes in the landscape, while others are surrounded by steep bluffs. Each lake has its own unique soil profile, moisture regime, and solar aspect that has determined the character of the plant communities that are present.

The other major factor that shapes the shoreline condition is human alteration of the landscape. Humans generally prefer open environments with good visibility and easy access to the water. Likewise, we tend to prefer sandy bottomed beaches without mucky aquatic vegetation underfoot. As a result human landscapes tend to be groomed to keep vegetation low and organized. These interventions naturally can have some negative consequences.

The existing condition of your shoreline provides the foundation for what interventions are possible or necessary. What follows are profiles of some of the most common vegetative and slope conditions present along Minnesota shorelines and a breakdown of the key issues that must be considered when designing a shoreline garden.

UNDISTURBED SHORELINE
a remnant landscape

This condition is quite prevalent in many rustic lakeside cabin settings in Minnesota. In this situation, intact woodland or grassland plant communities that have never been mechanically disturbed provide a range of stabilization, filtration, and habitat benefits. However, due to neglect and human use, these areas can often be compacted or infested with invasive species. It is important to protect these areas from any additional damage by planning human drainage and access to have as little impact as possible. Likewise, activities that will restore or enhance remnant natural areas can improve the resiliency of the shoreline. Unless significant erosion issues are present, it makes sense to avoid major disturbance of these areas.

Intact shorelines can be subtly managed to improve species diversity, control weeds, and add more color and seasonal interest.

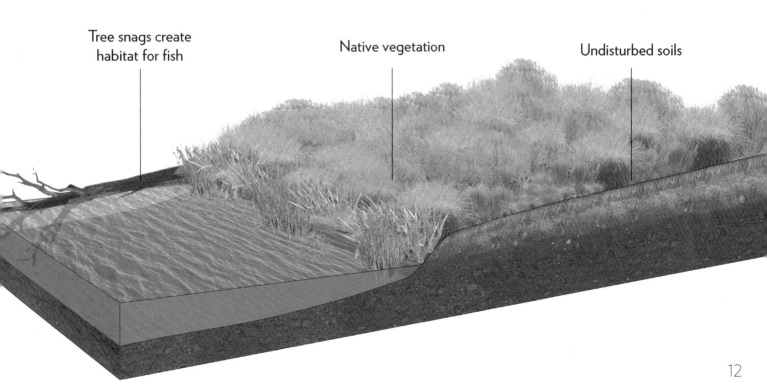

Tree snags create habitat for fish

Native vegetation

Undisturbed soils

INVASIVE SPECIES
an ecological threat

Invasive species such as reed canary grass, hybrid cattails, and purple loosestrife are widespread throughout Minnesota. They form dense colonies that will take over wetland and shoreline areas and will choke out other vegetation. Removing established colonies below the Ordinary High Water Level (OHWL) typically requires a permit from the DNR and must be completed by a licensed professional. This process often involves extensive herbicide application and mechanical removal and must be part of an ongoing effort in order to be successful. Likewise, these areas often do provide some water quality improvements and habitat value. Depending on the intensity of the infestation, the more practical approach is often to leave the invasive species present below the OHWL and focus on upland planting and maintenance strategies that will contain these species and fit with the overall landscaping scheme for the property.

Eradicating a patch of invasive species is a long term undertaking that can take years to complete.

Prolific seeding will spread to other areas

Aggressive monocultures form

Mowing will suppress invasion

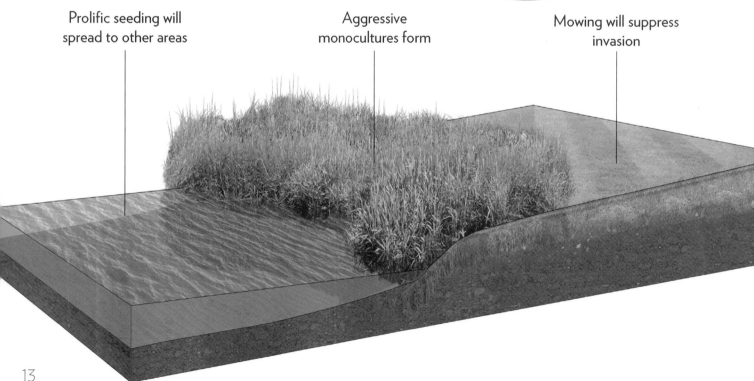

TURF SHORELINE
a common condition

Many property owners maintain a mown turfgrass lawn right to the edge of the water. Often times there are constraints near the shoreline such as tree roots, marshy soils, or steep slopes that make it challenging to mow all the way to the edge. This means that there is often a rough, rocky, weedy area just along the water's edge that has a greater risk of bank collapse. This situation, while quite typical, is problematic in that it results in minimal filtration of upland runoff, greater erosion risk, and increased loading of fertilizers and organic materials into the lake. Most varieties of turfgrass are not well suited to growing on wetland edges as they have shallow roots and do not handle saturation well. Taken together, this means that this condition is highly unsustainable and should be replaced with a more durable alternative as soon as possible.

Turfgrass is not well suited to growing near the water's edge. Its roots are typically too short to effectively stabilize the soil.

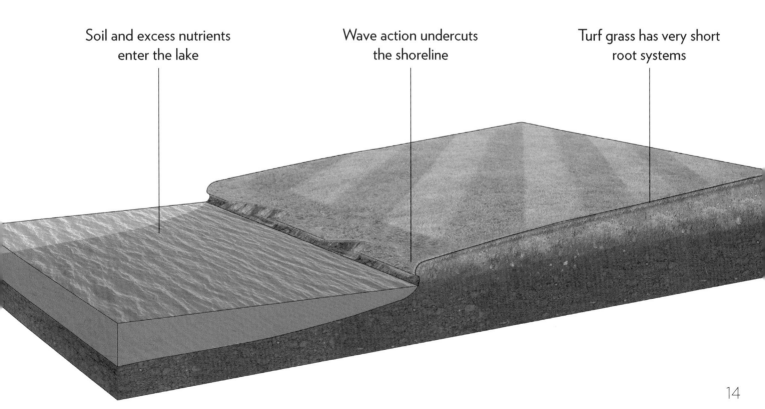

Soil and excess nutrients enter the lake

Wave action undercuts the shoreline

Turf grass has very short root systems

RIP-RAP
the conventional approach

Rip-rap is one of the most common methods of shoreline stabilization. Rip-rap or boulder armoring is a simple and low maintenance treatment that will stabilize the shoreline against wave action and minor ice heaving. The armoring typically starts below the Ordinary High Water Level (OHWL) and extends above the 100 year flood elevation. Installing rip-rap armoring typically requires a permit from the Department of Natural Resources, your local city, and/or watershed district. The downside to armored shorelines is that they have significantly less habitat value and filtration value than a vegetated shoreline, particularly if there is turf grass growing directly to the edge of the rip-rap. This situation is perfect habitat for Canada Geese, who tend to be a nuisance on most developed properties. For this reason, rip-rap should only be selected as a design choice if a planted shoreline stabilization is unable to withstand the forces arrayed against it.

Leave existing rip-rap in place if it is structurally sound. Simply plant a garden above it.

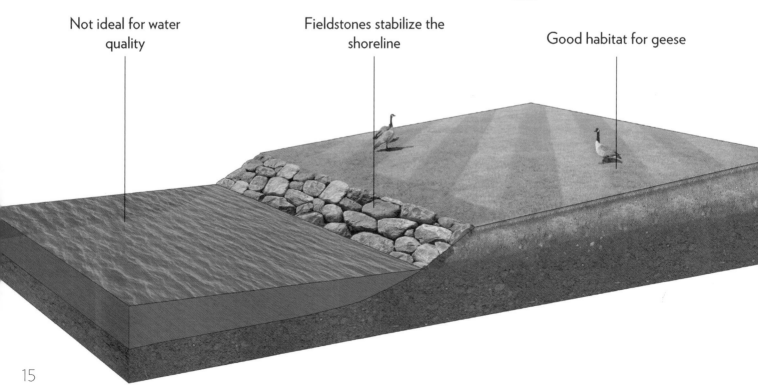

Not ideal for water quality

Fieldstones stabilize the shoreline

Good habitat for geese

Steep bluffs are a common condition around many Minnesota lakes, rivers, and streams. These areas are often left undisturbed during construction because of their extreme slope or as a result of protective land use regulations. These spaces are often negatively impacted by erosion from increased site runoff and invasive species infestation. If the area has been cleared of vegetation or replaced with turf grass, this intensifies the risk of bank collapse. It can be hard to establish new vegetation because of shade, poor soils, and the intense slopes. Due to these constraints, these areas are often left alone by property owners and over time can take on a feral character.

Mass plantings of vigorous species can stabilize slopes and be aesthetically pleasing.

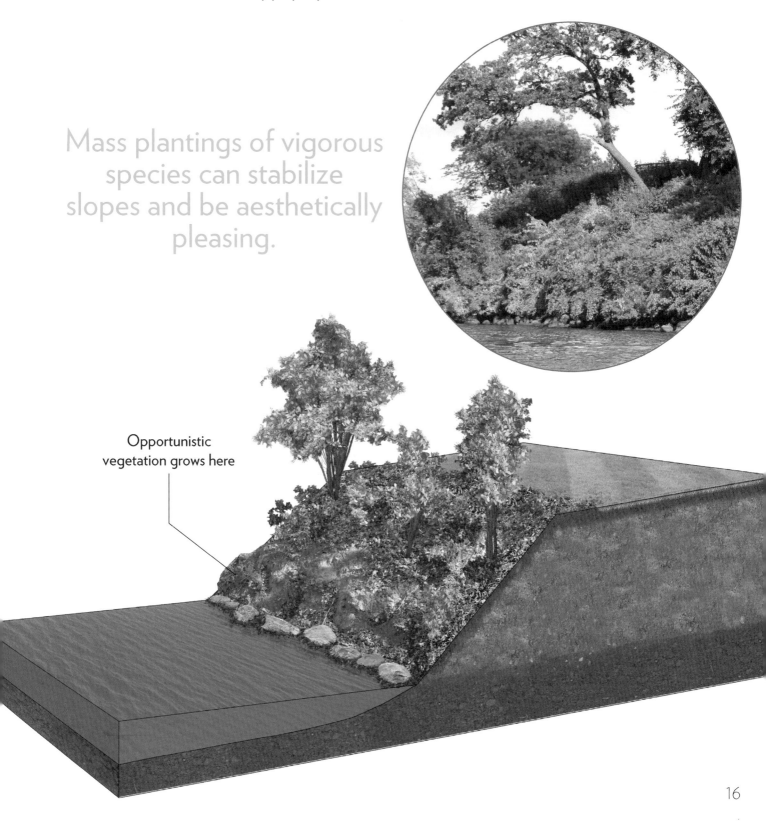

Opportunistic vegetation grows here

ICE RIDGE
a force of nature

Ice ridges are a natural form of land alteration resulting from the cracking and expansion of the ice sheet during the winter months. This is compounded by the force of wind pushing the ice sheet across the lake. This pressure pushes like a bulldozer, stripping away vegetation and churning up the shoreline. Depending on the intensity, this force can damage or destroy armoring or structures near the shore. When the ice recedes in the springtime, the resulting piles of bare soil are prone to erosion and may require regrading, armoring, re-vegetation, or other corrective action. In most cases this work will require a permit from the DNR, but the resulting landform and planting can also be designed as an attractive landscape feature that captures stormwater runoff and provides ecological benefits to the lake.

Ice ridges are a reminder of the sheer power of natural forces in the landscape.

Windward side of lake most vulnerable

Damage often requires annual repair

Upland runoff may be retained by berm

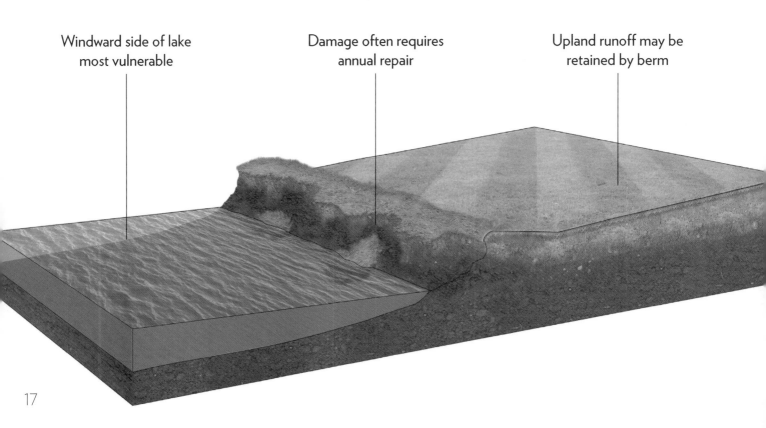

SANDY BEACH
a desired condition

Whether naturally occurring or man-made, beaches are an ideal spot for people to interact with the water. However these must be carefully designed or managed to prevent them from harming aquatic ecosystems, and may not be feasible in lakes with muddy bottoms. Creating a beach generally requires a permit and the DNR limits the amount of beach that can be created either as a result of filling or vegetation removal. In general, constructed beaches must be built according to local regulations and require ongoing maintenance to protect against degradation. Beaches are highly susceptible to erosion and are not appropriate in many shoreline contexts.

People love beaches. But they are one of the most high maintenance shorelines as they are highly susceptible to erosion.

Only occurs in sandy bottomed lakes

Vulnerable to wave action and erosion

Vegetation is often sparse

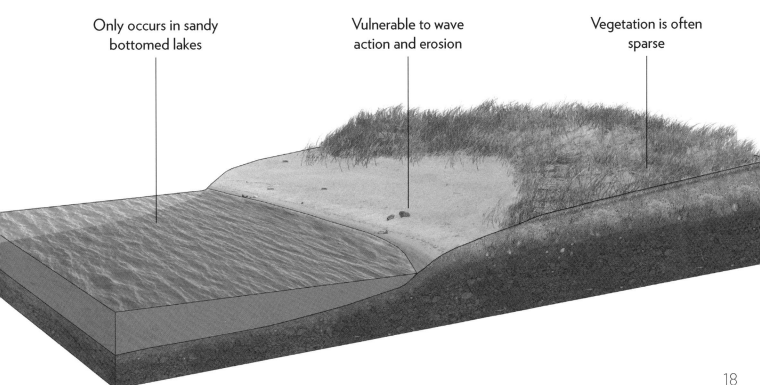

A diversity of shoreline conditions exist in Minnesota.

Some of them are the result of natural forces, but others were shaped by people. The shoreline condition informs what kind of garden will be possible on your property.

Gardens are shaped by a combination of human intent and natural process. Shoreline gardens can be dynamic improvements that serve important environmental functions while also being highly visible and beautiful.

Your shoreline garden is an expression of your relationship with the lake, but it also is a functioning part of the larger landscape. It can create wildlife habitat, enhance the architectural style of your home, or frame views to the water.

This chapter considers the range of design possibilities and outlines the critical aesthetic elements of shoreline gardens.

DESIGNING YOUR SHORELINE GARDEN

SHORE APPEAL
your second front yard

Creating curb appeal is a fundamental landscape design concept focussed on framing the views into the property from the street. Trees and garden spaces accent the architecture of the home and choreograph a pleasant arrival experience for visitors. The landscaping responds to the site and the architecture while having a sense of order and intent. Plant materials are selected for their seasonal interest and arranged to create a composed landscape space. Curb appeal is largely an aesthetic consideration, but it is a major driving force behind most private investment in urban landscapes.

There is a pressing need for the landscapes of the 21st century to transcend aesthetics. We must address a range of concerns that effect our way of life. The human transformation of the landscape has resulted in impairments to our water bodies, atmospheric pollution, and endangered wildlife populations. There is great demand for landscape practices that reduce our environmental footprint and begin to regenerate these natural systems. Overconsumption of groundwater aquifers means that landscapes should be designed to thrive without irrigation. The need to capture polluted stormwater runoff from developed landscapes has led to practices such as rain gardens and permeable pavements. There is a national effort to plant flowering species for pollinators such as bees and butterflies to counteract the precipitous decline in their populations over the last decade. In the context of climate change and ever increasing demands on limited natural resources, the traditional approach to landscaping has become inadequate. With our increasing awareness of the human impact on the earth, we must look for opportunities to address these global issues in our own backyards.

BEFORE

The shoreline garden presents such an opportunity.   Unlike traditional landscaping, a well-designed shoreline garden synthetically blends aesthetics and environmental functions to serve a vital purpose in the landscape. The shore appeal of a lake property is measured by these two factors. People not only perceive the visual appeal of your shoreline, they also see your commitment to stewardship.

By installing vegetation on your shoreline, you provide an environmental service to the lake. It now is up to you to decide what your shoreline garden should look like. Aesthetics are an essential component of sustainability. If a landscape is not attractive or meaningful to people, it will not be maintained or it will be removed entirely. There is a widespread assumption that the only acceptable shoreline improvement other than rip-rap armoring is native shoreline restoration, but in practice this is only one of many suitable planting design approaches. Native or wild plantings represent a particular aesthetic. Sustainability does not have a set aesthetic in the garden. It is about selecting plants that are well suited to the site, can be maintained with minimal inputs, and that improve the character of that particular place. By cultivating knowledge and an aesthetic sensibility, we can enhance the nature of our landscapes and form a new relationship with them.

"Our ability to perceive quality in nature, as in art, begins with the pretty." ALDO LEOPOLD

AFTER

THE SHORELINE GARDEN
a novel approach

A shoreline garden is a sustainable planting at the water's edge that stabilizes soil, filters runoff, provides habitat, and satisfies the aesthetic and maintenance preferences of its owner. So long as the shoreline garden follows the rules of thumb listed overleaf, the shoreline garden can be any style the property owner desires. It is important to remember that shorelines are more dynamic environments than traditional gardens. They must be able to withstand wave action, flooding, and other destructive forces. As a result, the selected plants must be adapted to tough conditions while also being attractive to humans. Enhanced Nature, a term popularized by the designers James Hitchmough and Nigel Dunnett, refers to a planting that values the importance of beauty for human users and recognizes that human created and managed landscapes can support considerable levels of biodiversity and perform critical ecological services. Shoreline gardens exemplify this approach to landscape design by integrating water quality and habitat performance goals with the need to accommodate human access and aesthetic preferences.

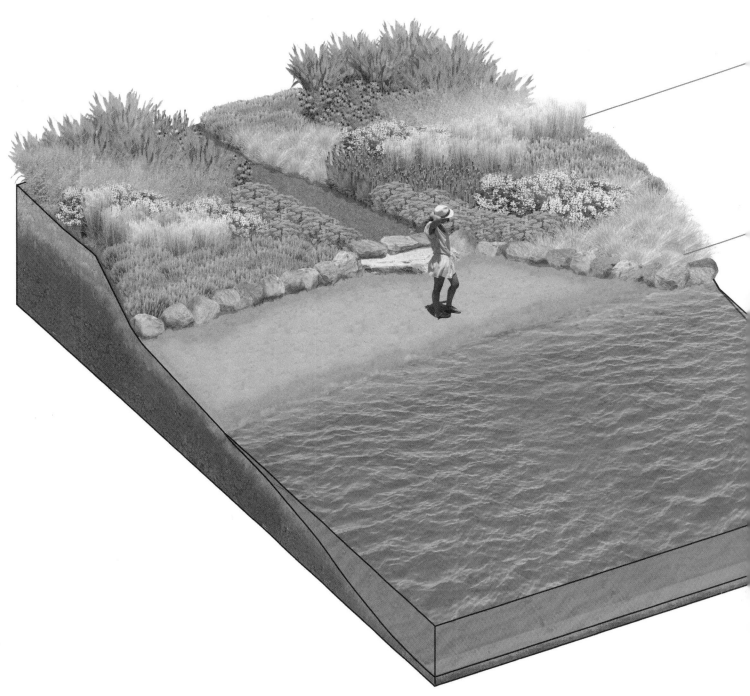

This rendering depicts a shoreline garden designed for visual interest and habitat value. Built upon a backbone of native plant species, the garden incorporates intermingled bands of cultivated native and introduced plant species to add color and contrast to the planting while at the same time increasing biodiversity and seasonality. The plantings will provide habitat for pollinators and bird species while having a striking floral display throughout the season.

The densely planted shore provides the important function of filtering stormwater runoff from the upland areas. A shoreline garden increases the absorbtion capacity of the soil and captures sediment and nutrients that otherwise would be washed into the lake. Having at least a twenty foot wide buffer strip along the shoreline will clean and filter the runoff before it reaches the water.

Whether by vegetative or structural means, creating a stable shoreline condition is critical to the success of any planting. This rendering shows an approach in which boulders are placed at the base of a planted slope to prevent erosion. What is most important is that erosion is eliminated and that wave action and ice heaving is absorbed. This stabilization can sometimes be accomplished with only vegetation, but may also require re-grading or structures.

Once established it is critical that the shoreline garden be maintained properly to prevent it from being overrun with weeds or invasive species. Having a maintenance plan is critical to keeping the garden in its desired state. By designing with management in mind it is possible to achieve a very low maintenance shoreline garden.

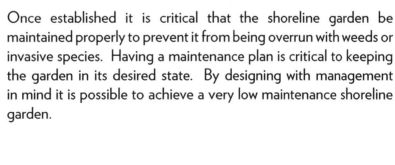

10 RULES OF THUMB
the basis for design

These rules of thumb provide a baseline set of standards that every shoreline garden should satisfy. These rules are essential to protecting the water quality of the lake. So long as these criteria are met, your shoreline garden can be designed to look however you like.

1 RESPECT THE RULES AND REGULATIONS

Cities and watershed districts have a legal responsibility to protect lakes and wetlands. When people fill in wetlands or disturb the shoreline they create problems for the community as a whole. Local regulations are designed to protect water quality and prevent the loss of flood storage space. In general, regulations protect existing shoreline vegetation and establish vegetated buffers. The chapter *Rules and Regulations* provides details on the design and permitting process for creating shoreline gardens.

2 STABILIZE THE SHORELINE

Erosion and bank collapse issues are the most catastrophic events for a shoreline both financially and ecologically. Regardless of the style of the proposed shoreline alteration, it must be designed to withstand the natural forces of the lake and keep soil and organic matter from being washed into the water by wave action or upland erosion. The *Stabilize Your Shoreline* chapter provides an introduction to the best practices for creating a stable shoreline using vegetation and structures.

3 PREVENT TRANSPORT OF ORGANICS TO THE LAKE

The shoreline garden should be designed to prevent organic debris and sediment from being washed into the lake from the upland areas of the property. This is best accomplished by installing proper erosion control during construction and by establishing a dense vegetative buffer.

4 RETAIN AND FILTER RUNOFF ON SITE

Design the landscape to maximize infiltration of rainwater. Route overland drainage through densely vegetated areas to maximize filtration. The more that the water can be slowed and retained by the landscape the greater the water quality benefits to the lake.

5 ELIMINATE INVASIVE SPECIES

Invasive species can rapidly infest your landscape. Be vigilant and eliminate them as soon as possible. The chapter entitled *Establishing Your Shoreline Garden* has profiles of several prominant invasive species and how they can best be managed.

6   AESTHETICS MATTER!

Determine how you want your shoreline garden to look prior to installation so that you can choose a plant palette and maintenance approach that will give you the desired aesthetic. The selection of plants and arrangement of materials can be designed to work with any style of architecture and landscaping. The chapter *Designing Your Shoreline Garden* presents different garden design alteratives for your shoreline.

7   DESIGN WITH HABITAT IN MIND

Protect areas on your property with habitat value and when possible choose species that will provide cover or food for wildlife. In general, shrubs provide cover and forage opportunities for birds, while bees and butterflies benefit from flowering perennials. Plants that provide habitat for birds and bees are identified in the *Shoreline Garden Plant Guide* chapter.

8   PROPER TURF MANAGEMENT

Reduce the amount of nutrient runoff generated by turf areas by maintaining a lush and healthy lawn with complete soil coverage. Never apply fertilizer within 20' of the shoreline. Set your mower deck to cut your grass blades to be 3" high. Turfgrass that is shorter will have a more shallow root system, require more irrigation, and is more susceptible to erosion.

9   USE HERBICIDES ONLY WHEN NECESSARY

Herbicides should only be used to control extremely aggressive weeds and should not be applied below the OHWL without a permit. It is important to select the right chemical and apply it correctly to control the target species without damaging the rest of the environment. The chapter entitled *Establishing Your Shoreline Garden* has specific recommendations for proper herbicide usage.

10   HAVE A MAINTENANCE PLAN

Every garden has unique maintenance needs. Develop a plan that is customized for your garden to keep it healthy and looking great. The chapter entitled *Establishing Your Shoreline Garden* provides a detailed breakdown of the steps necessary to maintain your garden throughout the season.

RETHINKING YOUR LAWN
why so much grass?

There is no secret why turfgrass is the most common land cover in the residential landscape. Turf is cheap and easy to install and when properly maintained, it provides a neat and clean appearance. It is important to remember that a turf space is an empty space. It might on occasion be needed to host activities and parties, but rarely is every area of a lawn used actively. Here is a simple test to determine if unnecessary areas of turf exist in your yard.

If you only go there to mow, it probably doesn't need to be lawn.

The pervasive use of turfgrass can cause several problems for the lakefront landscape. When turfgrass is improperly fertilized, grown right to water's edge, or allowed to erode it will result in a variety of unwanted consequences. First and foremost, all of these situations will encourage the movement of nutrients (primarily phosphorus and nitrogen) into the lake. This can create algae blooms, which upset the chemical balance of the water and can ultimately kill fish. Additionally, these actions will attract geese to your property.

When you have turfgrass right to the water's edge, you have effectively laid out the *green carpet* for geese to have a gala event on your lake shore. The geese will repay you by compacting your soil, slowly killing your turfgrass, pooping everywhere they can, and contributing an inordinate amount of nutrients to your lake. The best method of removing the invitation for geese to is to plant your shoreline with a garden. Vegetation at the waters edge triggers an instinctual response to stay away as predators commonly lurk in the vegetation near a shoreline.

Want to deter geese from your shoreline?
Replace the turfgrass with a garden

CONSIDERING VIEWS
balancing prospect and privacy

Great views are one of the primary benefits of owning a lakeshore property. When making changes to your lakeshore landscape, naturally one does not want to obstruct these views. This is often the first objection to planting vegetation at the lake's edge. However, in many cases vegetation can be used to enhance or focus views of the lake. Trees and shrubs can be utilized to screen neighboring houses, docks or other structures. They might also be used to focus attention on a particularly beautiful focal element such as an island or a summer sunset.

Vegetation can be placed carefully throughout your site to enhance the privacy of your lake home. The image below shows how trees and garden spaces have been placed to obscure the house from the lake and create privacy while still maintaining the outward views. Often, the initial impulse of lakeshore landscaping is to clear all vegetation to maximize the view of the lake. However, maximizing your views of the lake does not need to minimize your privacy.

You can plant your shoreline in a way that provides privacy while enhancing your view.

28

AESTHETICS
a continuum of style

formal   enhanced nature   wild

Shoreline gardens can be composed of both native and cultivated species

A shoreline garden is intentionally designed to add appeal to the property from both the land and water. Like all gardens, they exist on an aesthetic continuum. At one end of the spectrum there are formal gardens and at the other end are more wild or naturalistic plantings. This continuum speaks to the level of human control visibly evident in the planting. For instance, topiary gardens, like the one shown below on the left, represent the formal end of the spectrum where the landscape is precisely controlled through the careful manicuring of hedges. This planting style works well on open sites with formal architecture. Such a planting can still provide the same stormwater treatment and incorporate a carefully framed, but diverse perennial garden. At the other end of the spectrum are more wild gardens, like the native shoreline restoration shown below on the right. In these conditions the human imposed order is less apparent and the plants are allowed to intermingle, evoking wild nature. A shoreline garden can be planted as a native restoration, with an effort made to restore the aquatic and emergent plant communities as well as the upland species. This approach tends to work best in more undisturbed settings where it will enhance the existing plant communities and blend with the surrounding natural areas. In each case the goal is to design a resilient planting that is able to thrive in its shoreline context, improve biodiversity, and be appreciated and maintained by its human stewards. In the middle of the spectrum is the more balanced "enhanced nature" approach. What follows is a breakdown of the distinct planting styles that exist along the aesthetic continuum. Each profile includes example images and a diagram that communicate the thought behind the design approach.

SHORELINE CONTINUUM

29   formal   enhanced nature   wild

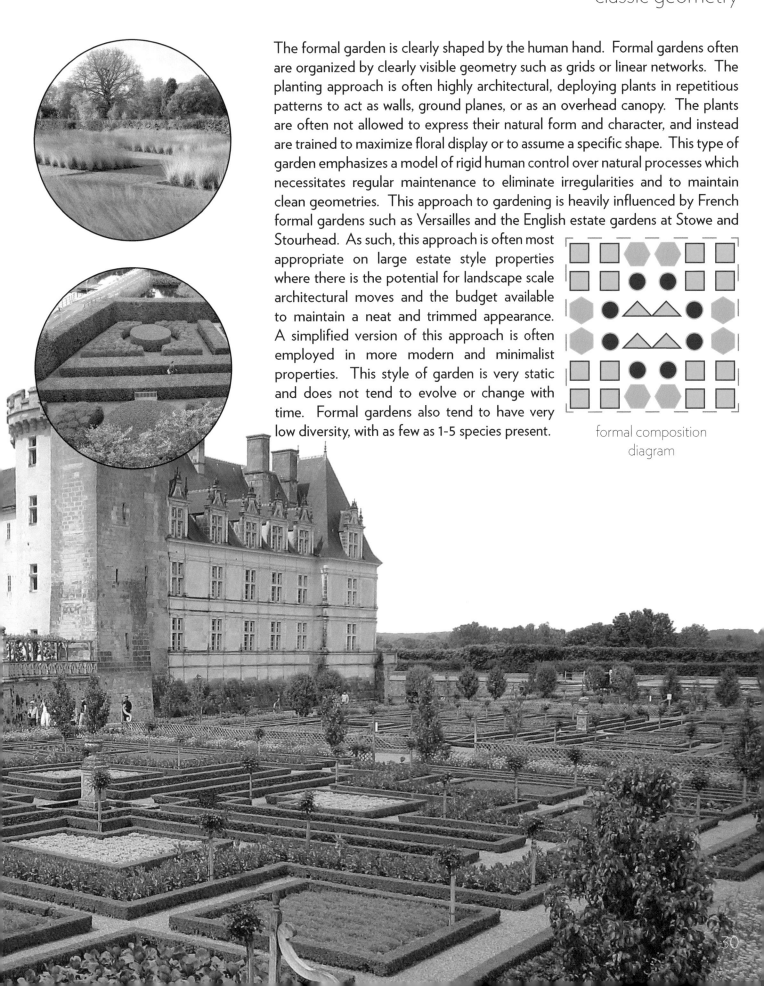

The formal garden is clearly shaped by the human hand. Formal gardens often are organized by clearly visible geometry such as grids or linear networks. The planting approach is often highly architectural, deploying plants in repetitious patterns to act as walls, ground planes, or as an overhead canopy. The plants are often not allowed to express their natural form and character, and instead are trained to maximize floral display or to assume a specific shape. This type of garden emphasizes a model of rigid human control over natural processes which necessitates regular maintenance to eliminate irregularities and to maintain clean geometries. This approach to gardening is heavily influenced by French formal gardens such as Versailles and the English estate gardens at Stowe and Stourhead. As such, this approach is often most appropriate on large estate style properties where there is the potential for landscape scale architectural moves and the budget available to maintain a neat and trimmed appearance. A simplified version of this approach is often employed in more modern and minimalist properties. This style of garden is very static and does not tend to evolve or change with time. Formal gardens also tend to have very low diversity, with as few as 1-5 species present.

formal composition
diagram

CONTEMPORARY
the suburban standard

The contemporary style is a landscape design approach grounded in the suburban American yard. It is largely about organizing trees, lawns, foundation plantings and perennial beds to complement the architecture of the home and define outdoor gathering spaces. The style often uses a curvilinear form vocabulary to soften the hard edges of the buildings and property boundaries. The planting approach creates small groupings of shrubs and perennials that are chosen as specimens for their flowers, massing, or texture. These plants are typically drawn from a list of horticultural standards that are known for their floral

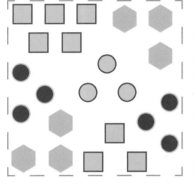

contemporary composition
diagram

display and reliability. These plants are spaced out and treated as individuals rather than as a massing. Aside from the growth and maturation of the specimens, this style of garden is relatively static. The overall diversity of the plantings tends to be on the low side with 5-10 plants present in the garden. This approach tends to be most effective on properties with an irregular mix of architectural styles and landscape conditions. It has the potential to unify inconsistent elements with relatively low maintenance and a tighter budget.

The new wave style is a European approach to garden design that has come to the forefront in recent years. Popularized by the Dutch garden designer and plantsman Piet Oudolf and his contemporaries, the new wave style emphasizes large drifts of monocultural plantings carefully arranged in loose and flowing geometries. The Lurie Garden in Chicago's Millennium Park is perhaps the most famous new wave garden in America. The style is an impressionistic reinterpretation of nature that creates striking plant combinations that remain interesting through the seasons. This approach is less concerned with flower color and more concerned with the form and appearance of the plant throughout its growth cycle. This style is largely focused on the use of perennials and arranges them to contrast the different species that are present and to show off the distinctive characteristics of each plant including how it reflects the light and moves in the wind. Often times the gardens contain a mix of horticultural specimens and native species. This style typically has moderately high levels of diversity with between 10 and 15 different species present. These gardens are usually managed much more loosely than a contemporary garden, allowing the planting to evolve and change over time. This style of garden works well in areas with a decent amount of open space, for example, as a replacement for a large lawn area.

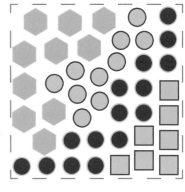

new wave composition
diagram

NATURALISTIC
the evocation of nature

The naturalistic garden is an evolution of the new wave style, that moves away from the large massings of plant material towards a stylized reflection of a wild plant community. This style is achieved by laying out overlapping matrices of grasses or perennials and then placing impromptu groupings of plants throughout the design. These informal clusters have an apparent randomness to them, but they are often the result of a modular and irregularly repeating templates. In this way, naturalistic gardens create a tension between order and disorder. These gardens often contain a mix of native and horticultural species and are allowed to migrate and

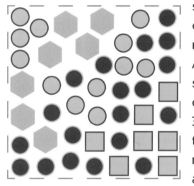

naturalistic composition
diagram

seed around, leading to a high degree of evolution over time. The High Line in New York City is the most famous example of a naturalistic garden in America. The plants are often selected for their seasonally dynamic qualities with a high level of diversity present throughout the garden, often 15-30 species. The gardens can largely be maintained through mowing, burning or other extensive control methods. This approach is often most effectively applied in transitional zones between landscaped and wild parts of a property.

WILD
a re-creation of nature

The wild style is the approach most often associated with natural resource restoration activities. This speaks to an effort to re-establish a native plant community on an altered site. This kind of garden is often established from seed or else is planted in large swaths using plugs or bare root stock. The human hand in this kind of planting is largely invisible once established, and plants in the garden typically seed around, colonize certain areas or die back depending on the seasonal conditions and microclimates. The plants selected for this kind of garden are predominantly native and are chosen based on their establishment patterns relative to the other species in the mix. The goal is to recreate a functioning plant community that is able to withstand invasive species infestation and will be maintained with an extensive burning or mowing regime. They are often chosen their effectiveness as habitat or for bioengineering purposes. This kind of garden often has very high diversity with 25+ species present. For a wild garden to be most effective visually, they require large spaces. Small wild gardens often appear weedy and unkempt.

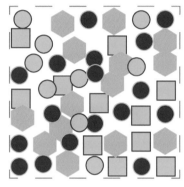

wild composition diagram

NATURALISTIC LAKEHOUSE
creating a feeling of pure nature

coconut coir blankets
and brush wattles
placed along slope
to control erosion

previous slope
showed signs of erosion

invasive species
treated and removed
prior to new plantings

shoreline vegetation
filters and cleans
runoff before it
enters the lake

CONTEMPORARY LAKEHOUSE
conversion of a large lawn to shoreline garden

shoreline vegetation
deters geese from
congregating

replace old dilapidated retaining
wall with shallow vegetated slopes,
increasing floodplain storage

rock gabion structures dissipate waves
and allow a high diversity shoreline
habitat zone to be created

rock gabion structures protrude no more
than 5' lakeward from Ordinary High
Water Level

The overarching objective of a shoreline garden is to replace turfgrass with a densely planted buffer strip.

Beyond this, the possibilities are endless.

Developing the vision for your shoreline garden is an essential early step in the process, but in order for the vision to be realized the garden must be able to withstand the array of human and natural forces that shaped the shoreline to begin with.

Shorelines are by their nature much more dynamic spaces than other parts of the landscape. As a result, shoreline gardens must be more adaptable and resilient than a traditional garden. This chapter will explore some of the forces that impact shorelines and some of the techniques you can use to create a shoreline garden that can thrive in this ever changing environment.

STABILIZING YOUR SHORELINE

DESTRUCTIVE SHORELINE FORCES
Understanding the forces that shape shorelines

EROSION

Bank erosion along shorelines is typically the result of concentrated stormwater flows from upland areas, or the result of wave action. Erosion is a natural consequence of water movement through the landscape. The increased amount of impervious surfaces and drainage infrastructure (storm sewers, agricultural drain tile, etc) results in flows with higher velocity and concentrations that can scour away established vegetation. Steep slopes and areas with minimal vegetative cover are most vulnerable to erosion. Erosion often starts small and then compounds over time as gulleys form or wave action undercuts the bank. Once bare soil is exposed the problem intensifies and typically requires regrading of the bank and some kind of structural or bioengineering solution to stabilize the slope.

WAVE ACTION

Wave action is one of the most omnipresent and destructive forces that shape shorelines. However, the intensity of wave action against a shoreline varies tremendously. The aspect, size, depth and topography of the lake can lead to dramatically different wave impacts. Human boating activity also will increase the intensity of wave action. The biomass of a well vegetated shoreline dissipates the energy of oncoming waves while the root systems help hold the soil in place. If the shoreline is stripped of vegetation and does not have armoring, wave action will scour away the bank over time. Whether the shoreline intervention is structural or biological, it must be designed to withstand the unique conditions of that site.

ICE HEAVING

Ice heaving is the most powerful destructive force that impacts shorelines in Minnesota lakes. Over the course of the winter the ice sheet on the top of lakes expands and contracts, creating cracks that then fill with water and freeze. As this process repeats the ice sheet steadily grows and begins to push like a bulldozer against the shoreline. This force has the ability to tear trees out of the ground and smash rip-rap armoring. The impact of ice heaving tends to be most dramatic on the windward side of lakes and is most dramatic in winters with rapid temperature fluctuations. In some cases, heavy armoring can withstand ice heaving, but in other situations the only solution is annual repair activities that must be permitted by the DNR.

SHORELINE ARMORING
Structural interventions to prevent shoreline scouring

Ideally, a shoreline can be secured exclusively with vegetation. This is the most ecologically beneficial option, but in some cases the forces impacting the shoreline exceed the stabilization capacity of plant material. In these instances, a structural approach to armoring the shoreline becomes necessary. The most commonly used option is rip-rap, a series of boulders placed into the shoreline to keep the soil from eroding away. Rip-rap has the advantage of being able to shift and settle in response to ice heaving or flooding, making it more resilient than most retaining walls. Likewise, it can be interplanted with wetland edge plants. Adding shoreline armoring will definitely require a permit from the DNR and usually cities and/or watershed districts as well. Below is a diagram illustrating the regulatory standards that typically must be met when constructing rip-rap along a shoreline. This diagram is not comprehensive and additional rules will apply by jurisdiction, so check with your local city or watershed district for guidance.

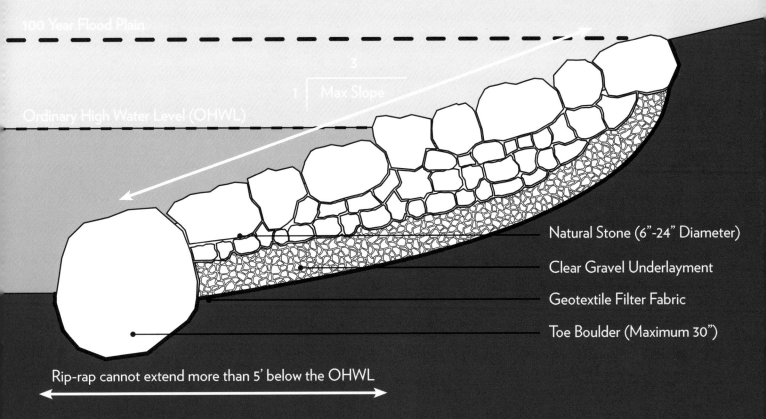

100 Year Flood Plain

3 / 1 Max Slope

Ordinary High Water Level (OHWL)

Natural Stone (6"-24" Diameter)

Clear Gravel Underlayment

Geotextile Filter Fabric

Toe Boulder (Maximum 30")

Rip-rap cannot extend more than 5' below the OHWL

In addition to rip-rap, it may also be necessary to armor the shoreline with a retaining wall or a sheet piling. The DNR discourages these approaches because the of their negative impact on emergent aquatic vegetation, and the potential for scouring at the base of the wall. It is never advisable to replace healthy, established shoreline vegetation with hard armoring. However, if there are significant erosion issues or the potential for structural damage, this kind of intervention can be justified. As with rip-rap, it will be necessary to seek construction permits. A range of design options for retaining walls exist that can armor the shoreline against destructive forces while also creating unique and memorable spaces.

EROSION CONTROL
keeping soil in place during installation and establishment

Installing a shoreline garden by its nature involves disturbing soil and vegetative cover in the vicinity of a water body. This alteration creates the potential for increased erosion and transport of sediment and nutrients into the water. As a result, it is essential that proper care is taken to stabilize the altered shoreline against wave action or stormwater runoff. Erosion control practices are typically specified and monitored by the city or watershed district and remain in place during the establishment period. Contact your local city or watershed district staff about local erosion control requirements.

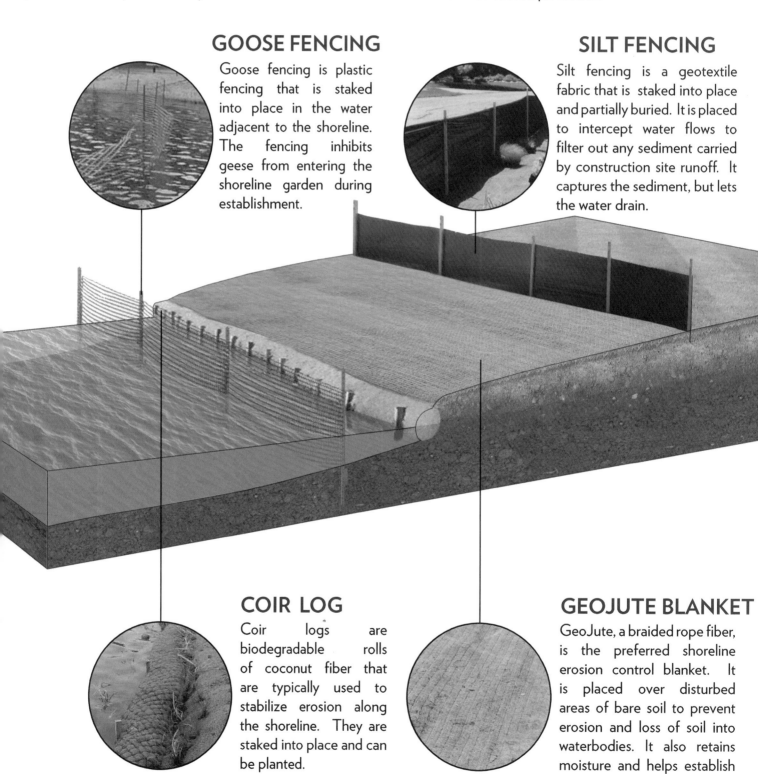

GOOSE FENCING

Goose fencing is plastic fencing that is staked into place in the water adjacent to the shoreline. The fencing inhibits geese from entering the shoreline garden during establishment.

SILT FENCING

Silt fencing is a geotextile fabric that is staked into place and partially buried. It is placed to intercept water flows to filter out any sediment carried by construction site runoff. It captures the sediment, but lets the water drain.

COIR LOG

Coir logs are biodegradable rolls of coconut fiber that are typically used to stabilize erosion along the shoreline. They are staked into place and can be planted.

GEOJUTE BLANKET

GeoJute, a braided rope fiber, is the preferred shoreline erosion control blanket. It is placed over disturbed areas of bare soil to prevent erosion and loss of soil into waterbodies. It also retains moisture and helps establish new plantings.

BIOENGINEERING
stabilizing shorelines with live plant materials

Bioengineering involves a range of practices that use the natural properties of plants, soil, and rocks to stabilize the shoreline. These practices typically involve structural assemblies of materials that rely on the living and growing properties of plants to lock soils into place over time. The techniques shown here are just two commonly used methods to stabilize steep slopes and to establish vegetation along shorelines. Determining the best bioengineering approach is a highly technical process. Consult a professional about the best approach for your site.

LIVE STAKES

Live staking is a quick and cost effective way to establish woody vegetative cover or to stabilize soil and create a low maintenance shoreline treatment. Live stakes are cuttings from a woody tree or shrub with its branches trimmed off so that it can be used as an anchor for erosion control blanket or planted into the gaps between rip-rap. A rooting hormone is applied to the stakes to encourage the growth of new roots from the cut. This method works best with specific species such as willows and dogwoods in wetland areas.

Brush fascines or wattles are a bioengineering technique that is most appropriate on steep, vegetated slopes. It involves tying together bundles of cuttings into fascines that can be staked into place to slow down concentrated flows of water and capture sediment. This approach is most appropriate in locations where the brush bundles can be harvested locally and the steepness of the slope renders erosion control blanket alone to be ineffective.

BRUSH FASCINES

SLOPE VEGETATION REMOVAL
removing vegetation without harming the site

Many Minnesota lakes have steep slopes along their edge. This condition results in an uninhabitable space between the water and the land. Due to neglect or disturbance, these areas are often overrun with invasive species and erosion. The process for improving these spaces involves careful removal of invasive trees and perennials while minimizing the mechanical disturbance of the roots and soil. A water safe herbicide is typically used to kill the plant. The upland portion of the plant is removed, while the root system is left in place. Then erosion control or bioengineering practices can be applied to the slope to stabilize it in preparation for replanting.

INVASIVE SPECIES

Buckthorn

Garlic Mustard

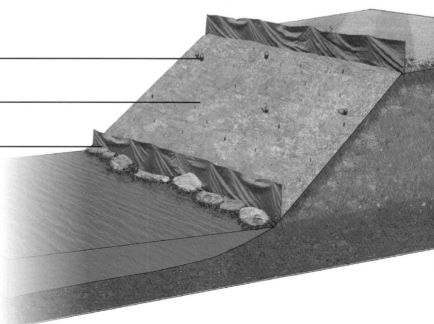

EROSION CONTROL

Herbicide Treated Stumps ————————

GeoJute Erosion Control Blanket ————————

Silt Fencing ————————

REPLANTING THE SLOPE
plants for tough spaces

Once the invasive species have been removed and erosion control is applied, it is necessary to plant replacement species that will be able to establish rapidly and compete with any invasive species that re-emerge. What follows are examples of different approaches to replanting that will result in an attractive shoreline that is low maintenance and able to compete with invasive species.

WOODY ORNAMENTAL

Serviceberry

Dwarf Bush Honeysuckle

GRASS MEADOW

Switchgrass

Bee Balm

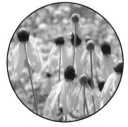

Yellow Coneflower

48

People alter shorelines.

It should always be done responsibly. In such a sensitive area, great care must be taken to make sure that there is no transportation of soils, sediment, or excess nutrients into the water body during the construction process or afterwards. Not only is this good practice, it also is essential to complying with the laws and regulations that protect the waters of the state.

Unlike traditional landscaping, shoreline gardens take place in an area of significant concern for state and local governments. Proactively communicating with these agencies is critical to understanding the rules and creating a streamlined approval process.

This chapter provides a brief overview of the different agencies that are responsible for monitoring shoreland alterations and lists some of the informational and financial resources that are available to help property owners improve their shorelines in ways that will benefit the larger lake ecosystem.

REGULATIONS AND RESOURCES

RULES AND REGULATIONS
shoreland regulatory agencies and critical thresholds

CITY GOVERNMENTS

Cities typically regulate site development and construction activities. Most also have standards concerning erosion control, stormwater management, and wetland protection. Often they will work with a local watershed district to establish and enforce local regulations.

DEPARTMENT OF NATURAL RESOURCES

The Minnesota DNR regulates the alteration of vegetation below the OHWL. To do so you must have an aquatic vegetation permit from the DNR and only Minnesota native plants may be planted.

The DNR also establishes shoreland management standards for public waterbodies that establish setbacks and other restrictions for lakefront development.

WATERSHED DISTRICTS

The Minnehaha Creek Watershed District issues permits for any shoreline alterations below the 100 Year Flood Elevation, including the installation of rip-rap armoring, bioengineering, planting or structural additions. The regulatory role of different Watershed Districts varies widely, but obtaining a permit is typically necessary.

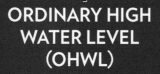

ORDINARY HIGH WATER LEVEL (OHWL)

The Ordinary High Water Level is the boundary of public waters or wetlands as evidenced by the presence of predominantly aquatic vegetation.

100 YEAR FLOOD ELEVATION

The 100 Year Flood Elevation is determined by FEMA and is an area adjacent to a water body that is subject to regional flooding events. This area should not be heavily disturbed.

Consult your local watershed district or city about your shoreline garden

The specific regulations that apply when creating a shoreline garden vary widely, so it is important to talk to the staff from your city or watershed district to get a full understanding of the rules. You may need to apply for a permit to perform certain actions. Up-front communication is important to preventing regulatory delays or punitive fines. The drawing below shows the areas of the shoreland that different agencies typically regulate.

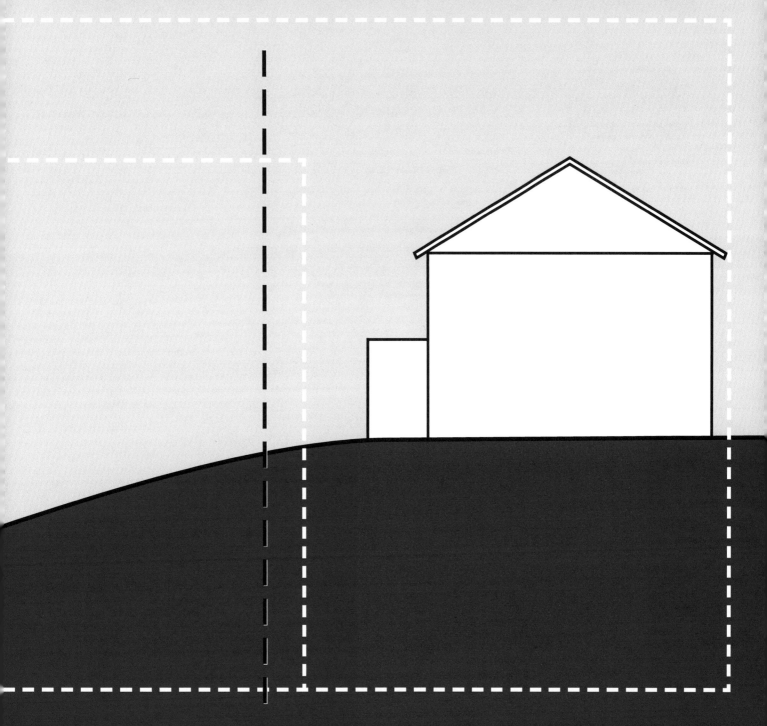

SHORELAND PROTECTION SETBACK

The shoreland protection setback is the area established by the DNR and the city government where it is not permissible to build structures or significantly regrade the site without a permit or variance. The setback varies by jurisdiction and activity.

COST SHARE GRANTS AND RESOURCES
public funding and support for private shoreline improvements

MINNEHAHA CREEK
WATERSHED DISTRICT

MINNEHAHA CREEK WATERSHED DISTRICT (MCWD)

The Minnehaha Creek Watershed District has funds available to help people install shoreline stabilization projects. Any property owner whose land is located within the boundaries of the MCWD can apply for a grant. For residential homes, the district will match up to $5,000 of design, construction, and maintenance expenses. For larger commercial or institutional projects there is no specified ceiling. It is possible to apply for shoreline grants all year round. Go to the website below for more information about the grant program.

Available Grants
http://www.minnehahacreek.org/grants

MINNESOTA BOARD OF WATER & SOIL RESOURCES (BWSR)

The Minnesota Board of Water & Soil Resources is the principal state agency dedicated to protecting Minnesota's soil and water resources. Its mission is to work in partnership with local organizations to provide funding, technical support, and programs that will enhance water quality and protect sensitive ecosystems. They have a resource page that is useful in identifying the local government agencies in your area which can provide resources or technical support when undertaking a shoreline garden project.

Local Government Units and Partner Agencies
http://www.bwsr.state.mn.us/partners/

MINNESOTA DEPARTMENT OF NATURAL RESOURCES (DNR)

If you are interested in managing aquatic vegetation below the OHWL or are interested in a more native aesthetic for your shoreline garden, the DNR has many excellent resources with more specific guidance about project planning, regulations, species selection, and proper installation techniques. The DNR resources listed below are useful sources for in-depth technical information.

Do I Need a Permit?
http://www.dnr.state.mn.us/permits/water/needpermit.html

Restore Your Shore
http://www.dnr.state.mn.us/restoreyourshore/index.html

Lakescaping for Water Quality
http://www.dnr.state.mn.us/eco/pubs_restoration.html

Once you have developed your shoreline garden design and have all the necessary permits, the next step is to install your garden and support it through the establishment period. This chapter will help you develop a greater understanding of the conditions that must be met for the garden to thrive along the water's edge.

ESTABLISHING YOUR SHORELINE GARDEN

BUILDING YOUR GARDEN
getting off to the right start

Your new garden is the beginning of a relationship.

Gardens are places where we direct the natural productivity of plants to make spaces that have purpose and meaning. As we have noted, people have the capacity to transform the landscape for our own ends. We can cut down trees to allow more sunlight to reach the ground. We can regrade the earth so that it is shaped according to our designs. We plant the species we like, where we want and provide the inputs they need to survive. Yet we still don't always get what we want. Despite our power, there are a multitude of forces at work that we need to acknowlege in order to effectively engage with the garden. Your relationship with your garden begins by paying attention to what it needs.

Plants need sunlight, water, oxygen, and nutrients to survive. Naturally, these elements are not always present on all sites in equal measure. As a result, different species have evolved to thrive amongst these diverse conditions. Many elements of your landscape are invisible and ephemeral. The micro-organisms in the soil and the fluctuations in microclimate can determine whether a garden is successful or overrun with weeds. A landscape wants to be something. Left to its own devices it will become a forest, a prairie, or perhaps a buckthorn patch. Its character is the result of its context, its natural tendencies, and of our actions within it. Some of these attributes are fixed, but some you can improve through strategic interventions in the landscape. The following pages outline a standard process for establishing and maintaining your garden. Done correctly, these actions will help your new garden get started on the right foot.

SITE PREPARATION:

The first step in creating a garden is to remove undesireable vegetation and install the proper erosion control measures. If you are removing a weedy area, mechanical removals can work but often require multiple attempts. Many weed species have the ability to resprout from tiny pieces of roots left in the soil. For this reason, chemical removals are typically most effective.

1. Layout the extent of your garden with paint or a garden hose

2. Install silt fencing to prevent soil from leaving the garden site.

3. Remove existing turf grass or vegetation. This can be accomplished through mechanical removal with a sod cutter, the application of a water safe herbicide such as Rodeo© or by smothering with a tarp.

SOIL AMENDMENT:

Gardens benefit from the addition of organic material to the soil profile. By tilling compost into the soil, you improve the drainage and moisture retention capacity of the soil. This creates an ideal condition for plant growth.

- Add 3" of organic manure or compost to your soil and mix thoroughly
- Don't use peat moss as its harvesting results in the destruction of boglands.
- Never add sand to your soil, especially with clay soils.

MULCHING:

A thick layer of mulch helps prevent weed establishment and helps retain moisture in the soil profile, it also helps to prevent soil compaction if laid prior to planting.

- Apply a 3" mulch layer in your garden prior to planting.
- Use shredded hardwood mulch rather than wood chips. It is widely available, made from local wood sources, as opposed to Cypress mulch that is harvested in the southern states.
- Do not pile the mulch around the crown of plants. This will suffocate them.

PLANTING:

The importance of properly planting the garden cannot be underestimated. Proper spacing, preparation, and installation will make sure that the plants have the best start possible.

- Layout the plants prior to planting to ensure correct placement and spacing
- Remove plants from container, water them, and gently break up their root balls.
- Dig the hole larger than the root ball (2x wide)
- Place plant into hole, leaving the top of the root ball above the soil level.
- Backfill the planting hole and press the soil firmly into place.

WATERING:

Watering is essential during the establishment period of a new garden. Water new plants for at least 4-8 weeks. Some plantings may need supplemental watering during times of drought.

- Water deeply and thoroughly. This means watering for longer and less often.
- Most plants do not like wet feet, especially when getting established. Do not over water.
- A general rule of thumb is 1-2" of water per week. Use a rain gauge to monitor this. Do not let an establishing garden go without water for more than 5 days.

SEASONAL MAINTENANCE
5 basic steps to keeping a healthy, beautiful garden

Maintenance is essential to a garden's long term success. Choosing the right plants is the first step, but proper care is necessary to make sure they establish as quickly as possible. The plants featured in this book are generally quite resilient and dependable, but all plants still need to be selected and placed in their preferred conditions.

Gardens can be high or low maintenance. This will largely be determined by the style of planting and the level of control that is desired. No landscape will ever be no-maintenance, but any landscape can be designed to require as little maintenance as possible.

The first two years of your new garden is the nurturing stage which will require a special kind of care. You will need to keep a watchful eye over the planting and make responsive adjustments.

Once your garden is officially past its initial nurturing stage, it is time to begin a more regular maintenance schedule. With five events each year, this basic schedule will guide you through the maintenance process and help keep your garden looking great. These steps can also be adapted based on the need for more rigorous weed control or additional watering during dry spells.

CUT BACK LAST YEAR'S GROWTH

All herbaceous perennials (non-woody plants) re-grow from ground every year. It is essential to cut back last year's growth of all perennials prior to any new spring growth. This will be the first major gardening activity of the season. The best time to do this is early spring when the snow has just melted and temperatures are warming. You can use a hedge trimmer, a string trimmer or even a lawn mower set high. Cut the plants to the ground and remove all of last year's growth.

PULL WEEDS
before Memorial Day
(cool season weeds)

The first weeding of the season is your chance to remove the early growing weeds before they set seed. These weeds typically seed around Memorial Day. Be sure to remove all weeds before then. Dandelions will be your best indicator. If they are setting seed, other cool season weeds likely are as well. Garlic Mustard, and Creeping Bellflower are also cool season weeds, but are best controlled chemically.

1. CUT BACK   **2. PULL WEEDS**

PULL WEEDS
before July 4th
(warm season weeds)

Your next weeding session will aim at removing the warm season weeds such as Thistles, Quackgrass and Foxtails. These weeds typically set seed around the Fourth of July. Thistles in particular are challenging to control with hand pulling and may need to be spot treated with herbicide.

WATER YOUR PLANTS

The late summer and early fall often brings extreme heat and prolonged periods of drought. This can be very stressful on garden plants, especially if the garden is not fully established. Pay close attention to your plants during this time. Giving your garden a deep and thorough watering during this time will go a long way in keeping your plants vigorous and healthy.

PULL WEEDS
around Labor Day
(warm season weeds
and tree seedlings)

The late summer and early fall also bring about more weeds to pull. This is a good time to identify tree seedlings that have established over the course of the growing season. Be sure to remove these now or they will be much harder to remove next year. Fall is also a good time to apply herbicides to noxious weeds and invasive species. Buckthorn is easiest to identify in the fall as the last plant with green leaves.

3. PULL WEEDS   4. WATER   5. PULL WEEDS

WEED CONTROL
best practices for controlling weeds and invasive species

The commonly accepted definition of a weed is a plant that is growing where you don't want it to be. In the context of a garden, this can mean species that are quite desirable in other places. What constitutes a weed will vary depending on the level of diversity and order present in the garden. Highly formal gardens will require regular weed control, while more informal gardens might be able to be managed more infrequently.

By contrast, invasive species or noxious weeds present a much greater threat. Invasive species have the potential to establish in contested spots and reproduce rapidly. If left unchecked they will displace desirable vegetation and form colonies that require extensive labor to eradicate. Therefore, the methods employed to control them must be capable of killing the entire plant as many invasive species have the capacity to regenerate from their roots. Regardless of the intensity of the maintenance regime, it is important to be on the lookout for invasive species in the garden. The following pages profile a few of the most commonly encountered invasive species and describe the best methods for eradicating them.

HAND WEEDING

Mechanical removal or hand weeding is the recommended approach to keeping unwanted weeds out of the garden, particularly during the first three years when the garden is getting established. Hand weeding is the most labor intensive approach to weed control. But if it is done regularly the presence of unwanted weeds will become less of a factor over time. When pulling weeds it is important to remove as much of the root system as possible and to limit the amount of bare soil exposed.

HERBICIDE APPLICATION

In general it is not advisable to spray herbicides in a garden setting. Aerosol drift from spraying can kill desirable plants and leave dead areas that will be vulnerable to new weed infiltration. Spraying is most appropriate in areas that are intended to be completely killed. The main reason to use herbicide in the garden is when noxious weeds are present and must be spot treated before they can spread. If you need to spot apply herbicide, mix a solution of glyphosate (aka Roundup©) in a no-spill container. Wear a pair of rubber gloves and pull over them a pair of absorbent cotton gloves. Cutting the tips of the cotton glove's fingers can help the fit. Saturate the cotton glove with the herbicide solution, squeezing out the excess so that it doesn't drip. Grab the leaves and stem of the targeted plant, applying the herbicide to that plant only. Do not touch adjacent desirable plants or they will be killed.

There are weeds and there are invasive species.
Big difference.

INVASIVE SPECIES CONTROL
Common Buckthorn, *Rhamnus cathartica*

Buckthorn Colony

Buckthorn Berries

Buckthorn Leaf

Buckthorn is an aggressive forest understory tree that forms dense thickets in woodland areas and outcompetes native forest understory and ground plane species. It seeds prolifically, grows quickly and retains its leaves late into the fall. The presence of Buckthorn leads to a dramatic drop in forest understory diversity and requires ongoing management. Both European and Glossy Buckthorn varieties are widespread throughout Minnesota and are considered invasive species.

MECHANICAL CONTROL

Two principal methods of mechanical control exist. For new whips less that 3/8" in diameter, one can use a tool called a weed wrench to pull the entire plant out of the ground. In areas with erosion potential do not remove the root system to avoid exposing bare soil. For larger specimens, the Buckthorn must be cut down to the stump. This can be accomplished with a chainsaw for larger specimens or by using a brush saw. This approach is most effective if herbicide is applied immediately after the cut.

CHEMICAL CONTROL

Chemical treatment is best done in conjunction with cutting. The best time to cut and treat Buckthorn with herbicide is in late September through November. Once the stump has been cut apply Ortho Brush-B-Gon© (active ingredient Triclopyramine) immediately to introduce the herbicide. It is most important to apply the herbicide to the outer 2-3 inches of the stump if it is larger than 6 inches in diameter.

REPLACEMENT PLANTING

Once Buckthorn has been removed it is critical to plant other shrubs in its place that can successfully compete with it. Woodland shrubs like Dogwoods or Viburnums are recommended replacements.

Weed Wrench

Brush Saw

INVASIVE SPECIES CONTROL
Reed Canary Grass, *Phalaris arundinacea*

Reed Canary Grass Seed Head

Reed Canary Grass Colony

Reed Canary Grass (RCG) is an invasive perennial cool season grass that is known for its ability to aggressively colonize wetlands and outcompete native wetland species. Reed Canary Grass is a Eurasian species that has been planted around the country since the 1800s to serve as a forage crop and for erosion control purposes. It has since naturalized. It reproduces by sending out rhizomes, which are horizontal growths that form a dense mat. These stands thrive in areas of soil disturbance, but also will opportunistically invade intact wetland communities. Reed Canary Grass is also a prolific seeder, shedding thousands of seeds during a typical growing season. These seeds can be carried downstream to new locations where they will establish new colonies. Once established, it produces a seed bed which will allow it to rapidly regenerate even if the existing colony is removed. These traits make it incredibly challenging to remove once established. Consult with a professional about the best approach to treating the grass as you will most likely need an aquatic vegetation permit from the DNR to remove and replace it.

MECHANICAL CONTROL

The most common mechanical control method is to cut RCG down in June and October to prevent it from setting seed. Most other mechanical removal methods involve substantial disturbance of the wetland edge and are therefore not recommended, particularly as there is great potential for RCG to reestablish from seed. Likewise, most purely mechanical methods are more likely to just slow the spread of RCG rather than eradicating it.

CHEMICAL CONTROL

The most effective approach to eradicating reed canary grass is to apply herbicide to the leaves of RCG in the springtime before other native wetland species emerge. This will kill the plant down to the roots, but it will still likely take several applications to completely eradicate the entire stand. The Minnesota DNR recommends using Rodeo©, a formulation of glyphosate, that is approved for use in wetland environments. Once the herbicide has taken effect, the plant will dry out and can be cut back or burned.

REPLACEMENT PLANTING

There are very few native plant species that are robust enough to take the place of RCG and hold their ground against renewed infestations. The primary contenders are Prairie Cord Grass (*Spartina pectinata*), Bluejoint Grass (*Calamagrostis canadensis*) or Lake Sedge (*Carex lacustris*).

INVASIVE SPECIES CONTROL
Garlic Mustard, *Alliaria petiolata*

Garlic Mustard - Year One

Garlic Mustard - Year Two

Garlic Mustard is an invasive Eurasian biennial species that spreads both rhizominously and by seed. In the first year, it spreads like a low ground cover through rhizomes. In the second year it sends up a single stem that is 12-36" tall and produces seed. It is most often encountered in disturbed forest areas, but it is capable of spreading into intact forest areas and displacing native herbaceous plants. It is one of the first herbaceous plants to emerge in the springtime and persists into late fall. If it is allowed to persist, it will form dense colonies that will outcompete nearly all forest ground plane species. It is one of the most challenging and persistant invasive species and the removal process will likely be ongoing even if a localized infestation is eradicated.

MECHANICAL CONTROL

Garlic Mustard is nearly impossible to control through mechanical means alone. Hand pulling is largely ineffective, although mowing prior to it setting seed can slow the rate of infestation. Mowing after the plant has set seed will result in the seed being broadcast throughout the area and can cause additional infestation. Once the plant has set seed for the season, it must be physically bagged and removed from the site or else it must be burned to prevent the seed from spreading further.

CHEMICAL CONTROL

The most effective method for treating Garlic Mustard is to spot apply glyphosate in the early spring or late fall when other herbaceous plants are still dormant. Given the enduring presence of Garlic Mustard in the seed bank, this process will likely need to happen on more than one occasion.

REPLACEMENT PLANTING

Garlic Mustard should generally be replaced by other aggressive forest understory species to prevent re-emergence from seed. The primary contenders are Canada Anemone (*Anemone canadensis*), Pennsylvania Sedge (*Carex pennsylvanica*), and Big Leaf Aster (*Aster macrophyllus*).

Thoughtful site preparation is an essential foundation for a successful shoreline garden, but that is just the beginning. Having a regular maintenance regime for your shoreline garden is the best way to ensure that it looks and functions as intended in the long term. Spending time in your garden and getting to know the different plants is a great way to build appreciation for your lake shore and to truly make it your own.

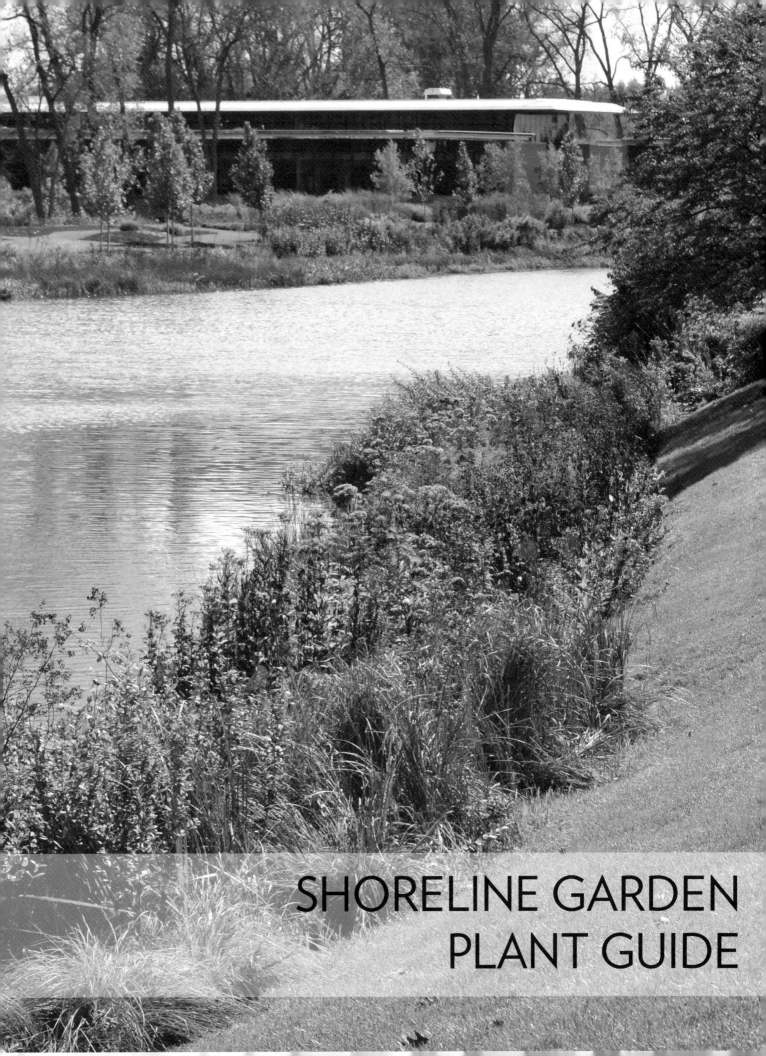

SHORELINE GARDEN
PLANT GUIDE

PLANT SELECTION
understanding the intrinsic qualities of plants

The plants you choose will define your garden.

Plants are the actors, the characters, and the personality on the stage that is the garden. The type of plants, the way they relate to one another, and the way they are placed in the landscape will establish the style that your garden communicates. The associations your plants have with animals and insects will determine your garden's relative habitat value. The ability of plants to respond and adapt to site conditions will determine your garden's overall health and vigor. Collectively, these factors will define the functional success and visual appeal of your garden. The primary and paramount decision with any garden design is: "What plants should I use?" This is obviously a very difficult and potentially burdensome challenge. The variable site complications and nearly infinite plant species to choose from are enough to mystify and frustrate anyone. The following pages attempt to simplify this troublesome issue and provide techniques and suggestions for navigating the complex world of plant selection.

Horticultural cultivation has introduced a perplexing division in garden design.

The advances of horticultural science have allowed us to cross-pollinate, hybridize new species, genetically modify, and reproduce desirable traits within nearly any plant. This scientific revolution has introduced compelling and sometimes bizarre new plants. Many horticultural innovations become so popular they proliferate across the planet and traditionalize as landscape commodities. A landscape wholly comprised of Daylillies, Hostas, or Spireas can be visually stale and typically provides little habitat. What is important to remember, however, is that these species became traditional for a reason. They are reliable, resilient, and very low maintenance. They rarely require fertilizer, irrigation, or much of any kind of input. These are highly desirable traits of any plant species and ultimately traits of sustainable landscapes. However, these plants have been overused to the point that they have lost their identity or become "nowhere plants." This issue, in combination with the rampant destruction of remnant natural areas, has popularized the use of native plants in the built landscape. Native plants present a unique opportunity to instill a sense of regional identity into a landscape. A prairie garden can be emblematic of the tallgrass prairie that once covered the great plains. Woodland ephemeral flowers can be planted in your shade garden to emulate a forest. While native plants can provide unique qualities to a garden, they are not always well suited to built landscapes. Native plants are often branded as more "sustainable" or "better for the environment". This can be true, but it is a generalization and over-simplification of a very complex situation. What is more accurate is to understand that all plants play a critical role in the ecological and natural processes of the earth. Regardless of a plant's origin, a gardener must choose the right plant for the right place.

What aesthetic style have you chosen for your garden?

All plants have an identity and personality. Their individual habits, forms, seasonal characteristics collectively contribute to broadcast a core essence. As such, a garden hoping to convey a particular style must be composed of plants communicating qualities emblematic of that style. A wild garden should be comprised of plant species that have a wild character. This might mean they have a looser form or that variation appears within different plants of the same species. Formal gardens will conversely utilize plants that exhibit uniformity and predictability. These qualities lend themselves better to forming monocultural blocks employed to articulate geometric structures and patterns. We are drawn to certain plants because of their intrinsic qualities. The plants we choose embody our tastes and inspirations.

Your garden is a living manifestation of what matters to you.

BUILDING COMBINATIONS

Plant combinations are the basic building block of the garden. A visually striking garden is composed of plant combinations that offer contrast and dynamism throughout the year. In order to create eye-catching combinations you must start to look differently at plants. See them less for their bright colors and more for their forms, structures, and seasonality. One effective way of doing this is to think in black & white and see leaf texture and flowers for their basic forms. The diagrams below separate leaf texture into three categories and flower form into six distinct groups. By building combinations of flowering perennials with differing flower forms and leaf textures, you will automatically instill contrast and seasonal interest.

LEAF TEXTURE

fine   medium   coarse

FLOWER FORMS

umbel

Yarrow, Joe-Pye Weed, Sedum, Golden Alexanders

daisy

Coneflower, Black Eyed Susan, Asters, Sunflowers

plume

Astilbe, Korean Reed Grass, Queen of the Prairie

spire

Blazing Star, Salvia, Anise Hyssop, Wild Indigo, Beardstongue

globe & button

Bee Balm, Allium, Globe Thistle, Rattlesnake Master

screen

Grasses, Prairie Dropseed, Switchgrass, Arkansas Blue Star   66

SHORELINE PLANTING ZONES
the right plant in the right place

Understanding the hydrologic regime is critical to making a successful shoreline garden. Your shoreline's steepness, soil condition, and position relative to the water table all impact the ability of plants to survive. Take some time to understand the basic soil moisture conditions that exist along your shoreline. This will provide important insight toward properly selecting plants for your garden. This cannot be overstated. If a plant that prefers dry, well-drained soils is planted right next to the water in what would be considered a wet, poorly-drained condition, then that plant will not grow properly or may die. Not only are you selecting plants for a garden, which can be a difficult task, you are selecting plants for a garden with a variable moisture gradient.

The ultimate success of a shoreline garden planting depends on selecting the right plants for the moisture conditions.

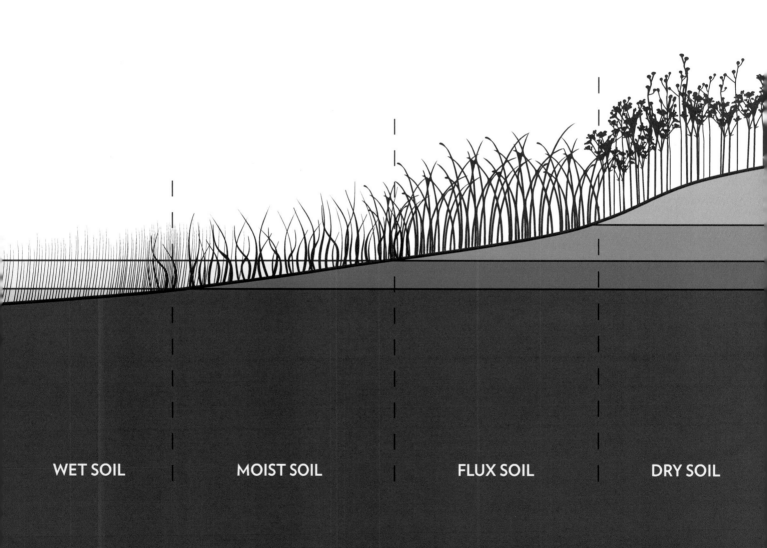

WET SOIL | MOIST SOIL | FLUX SOIL | DRY SOIL

HOW TO USE THE PLANT GUIDE

The following plant guide will aid you in selecting plants for your shoreline garden. The plant guide is broken out into three discrete sections: Flowering Perennials, Ornamental Grasses, and Shrubs. Each section is color coded as seen below.

| Flowering Perennials | Ornamental Grasses | Shrubs |

SUN

FULL SHADE

Plants adapted to a full shade condition receive less than 4 hours of direct sunlight per day

PART SHADE

Plants adapted to part shade typically receive 4 hours of direct sunlight per day

FILTERED SUN

Plants adapted to filtered sun condition will often be located near trees that provide light shade for part of the day

FULL SUN

Plants adapted to a full sun condition require at least 6 hours of direct sunlight per day

SOIL

WET SOIL

Plants adapted to wet soil are plants that are capable of surviving in standing water for extended periods of time

MOIST SOIL

Plants adapted to a consistently moist condition. Surface may be soggy after rains or during the spring melt

FLUX SOIL

Plants that can survive periods of moist and dry soil. These are very useful for shoreline gardens as soil conditions often fluctuate

DRY SOIL

Dry soils are at least 3' higher in elevation from the lake level. Plants adapted to dry soil do not like wet feet and require good drainage

ATTRIBUTES

POLLINATOR ATTRACTOR

These plants attract pollinators such as butterflies, bees, and ants. This is a critical ecosystem function

FALL COLOR

These plants turn vibrant colors in the fall. Adding a new dimension of seasonality to the garden

BIRDS & WILDLIFE

These plants attract birds and other intersting wildlife such as hummingbirds and songbirds

FLOWERING PLANT

These plant produce flowers that are attractive and interesting

WINTER INTEREST

Plants that can produce interesting effects during frost and winter periods of the year allowing enjoyment of your garden year-round

EROSION CONTROL

These plants are capable of colonizing and holding steep banks that might otherwise erode

LOW MAINTENANCE

These plant require little care outside of establishment or annual spring clean up

TOUGH SOIL BUSTER

These robust plants have the capability of growing in tough, compacted soils and still surviving

Anise Hyssop
Agastache foeniculum 'Blue Fortune'

AVERAGE DIMENSIONS
24-30" w x 24-36" h

FLOWER TIME:
June-September

VARIETY:
'Blue Fortune'

DESCRIPTION:
Blue Fortune Anise Hyssop is a tough and very attractive perennial. It blooms profusely for nearly 3 months provided it has enough sunlight. Given its long bloom time, this plant is a must for any garden hoping to attract pollinators. Although Anise Hyssop is tolerant of moist conditions, it prefers drier, well-drained conditions. The vertical, spike flower means that if pairs well with daisy-like and umbel flowers such as Asters, Black Eyed Susans, Coneflowers, and Sedums.

Arkansas Blue Star
Amsonia hubrichtii

AVERAGE DIMENSIONS
24-36" w x 30-36" h

FLOWER TIME:
May-June

DESCRIPTION:
The Arkansas Blue Star is a graceful and long-lived perennial that is best known for its fine foliage, steely blue flowers, and vibrant fall color. Spring flowers last through early June leaving a fine-textured foliage mound. Plant in large masses to create dramatic, bold gestures in your garden. Requires little care after initial establishment, which can be slow. Although the Blue Star can withstand moist soils, it prefers well drained conditions, so avoid saturated lakeside conditions. This plant will have golden fall color and thrive in full sun.

SUN

FULL SUN · FILTERED SUN

SOIL
EACH SPECIES HAS UNIQUE SOIL REQUIREMENTS

ATTRIBUTES

POLLINATOR ATTRACTOR · FLOWERING PLANT · LOW MAINTENANCE

Milkweed
Asclepias spp.

DESCRIPTION:

The Milkweeds are an ecologically critical plant. Despite the word *weed* in the name, not all Milkweeds should be treated as such. The common Milkweed has *weedy* tendencies, but each species plays a critical role in the garden. These plants are the host to Monarch Butterfly larvae. Given the decline of the Monarch population over the past two decades, planting milkweed in your garden is an important step in creating a haven and habitat for this important insect and pollinator. Apart from their ecological value, the Milkweeds are visually interesting and an excellent addition to the shoreline garden.

Butterfly Milkweed
Asclepias tuberosum

AVERAGE DIMENSIONS
12-18" w x 18-24" h

FLOWER TIME:
June-July

Perhaps the best Milkweed for the garden, Butterfly Milkweed needs dry, well-drained soil. Brilliant orange flowers emerge in June.

Marsh Milkweed
Asclepias incarnata

AVERAGE DIMENSIONS
18-24" w x 36-48" h

FLOWER TIME:
July-August

Marsh Milkweed is a moisture loving Milkweed but can grow in fairly dry soils as well. This will re-seed and move around in the garden. Great fall and winter interest.

Common Milkweed
Asclepias syriaca

AVERAGE DIMENSIONS
9-12" w x 24-36" h

FLOWER TIME:
June-August

Common Milkweed is somewhat weedy in its character and is not very handsome. However, if this plant finds its way into your garden, consider leaving it in place for Monarchs.

70

Aster

Aster spp.

AVERAGE DIMENSIONS
24-30" w x 24-36" h

FLOWER TIME:
June-September

DESCRIPTION:
Asters are flowering perennials that often produce prolific flowering displays. The Aster family *Asteraceae*, sometimes called the daisy or sunflower family, is huge, containing nearly 23,000 different species worldwide. Many species are well suited to the conditions of the shoreline garden. Most Asters are late season bloomers, many of which will bloom until the first frost. Nearly all Asters will attract pollinators such as bees and butterflies.

Purple Dome Aster
Aster novae-angliae 'Purple Dome'

AVERAGE DIMENSIONS
24-30" w x 24-36" h

FLOWER TIME:
Late August-October

This popular variety forms a tight dome shape that is covered with purple blooms. Can tolerate fairly moist conditions.

New England Aster
Aster novae-angliae

AVERAGE DIMENSIONS
24-30" w x 24-36" h

FLOWER TIME:
September-October

The native version of the Purple Dome. Grows much taller and has a tendency to flop over.

Woods Series Aster
Aster 'Woods Purple-Blue-Pink'

AVERAGE DIMENSIONS
12-18" w x 12-18" h

FLOWER TIME:
September-October

A very compact form that is best used in large masses. Prefers dry to medium soil moisture. Excellent disease resistance.

SUN

PART SHADE | FILTERED SUN | FULL SUN

SOIL

DRY SOIL

ATTRIBUTES

POLLINATOR ATTRACTOR | FLOWERING PLANT | LOW MAINTENANCE

Wild Indigo
Baptisia australis

DESCRIPTION:

A large shrub-like perennial that produces tall racemes of deep blue flowers in May. Extremely drought tolerant, Wild Indigo is a nitrogen fixing plant and is well suited for dry, poor soils. Wild Indigo is slow to mature, sometimes taking years to develop its deep root system. Avoid transplanting as this will disrupt it slow growing roots. Many cultivated varieties are available, each with a variation on the flower color. White, maroon, and deep purple varieties exist.

AVERAGE DIMENSIONS
36-48" w x 36-48" h

FLOWER TIME:
May-June

VARIETY:
'Purple Smoke'

SUN

FULL SHADE | PART SHADE | FULL SUN

SOIL

MOIST SOIL | FLUX SOIL | DRY SOIL

ATTRIBUTES

POLLINATOR ATTRACTOR | FLOWERING PLANT | LOW MAINTENANCE

Turtlehead
Chelone lyonii 'Hot Lips'

DESCRIPTION:

Turtlehead is a performer in the shoreline garden. Its ability to grow in sun or shade and love of moist soils make Turtlehead adaptable to most shoreline conditions. Best known for its dark, lustrous foliage and rosy pink snapdragon-like flowers, Turtlehead will add visual interest to any planting. For best results, plant in moist, rich soil with filtered light. Early season growth is a dynamic bronze green. Pinch back terminal buds early in the season if you wish to keep the plant shorter than its typical height.

AVERAGE DIMENSIONS
18-30" w x 24-36" h

FLOWER TIME:
August-September

Coneflower
Echinacea spp.

DESCRIPTION:

Another member of the Aster family, Coneflowers are a dramatic yet reliable perennial. This tried and true perennial is a mid summer stunner and a butterfly magnet. Echinacea is native to meadows and prairies of the United States and prefers well drained conditions. For an interesting change, try the Pale Purple Coneflower, a slender stemmed relative of the Purple Coneflower. It blooms earlier in the summer and has slender petals that hang down toward the stem. Many cultivars exist like the popular 'Magnus'. 'Prairie Splendor' is an exciting, new variety that is shorter and has a raspberry color bloom.

Purple Coneflower
Echinacea purpurea

AVERAGE DIMENSIONS
18-24" w x 24-36" h

FLOWER TIME:
Late June-August

A popular garden standard that is native to the midwestern prairie.

Prairie Splendor Purple Coneflower
Echinacea purpurea 'Prairie Splendor'

AVERAGE DIMENSIONS
18-24" w x 18-24" h

FLOWER TIME:
June-September

A short variety that features a deep raspberry color flower.

Pale Purple Coneflower
Echinacea pallida

AVERAGE DIMENSIONS
12-18" w x 24-36" h

FLOWER TIME:
June-July

This lesser known species of Echinacea is an early summer bloomer that has slender petals that hang from the tall, narrow stem.

SUN

FULL SUN | FILTERED SUN | PART SHADE

SOIL

MOIST SOIL | FLUX SOIL

ATTRIBUTES

POLLINATOR ATTRACTOR | BIRDS & WILDLIFE | FLOWERING PLANT | LOW MAINTENANCE | TOUGH SOIL BUSTER

Joe-Pye Weed
Eutrochium spp.

DESCRIPTION:

Joe-Pye Weed is a bold and beautiful perennial that typically grows along lake shores and riverbanks in robust fashion, making it a perfect choice for a shoreline garden. Large umbels of pink flowers atop red stems with whorled leaves bloom from July to September. Native species are often very large (sometimes 6-8' tall!) and may not be appropriate for every garden. However, many cultivated varieties exist which are shorter. Joe-Pye Weed is a magnet for pollinators, particularly Tiger Swallowtail butterflies. Pairs well with coneflowers, black eyed susans, and ornamental grasses.

Sweet Joe-Pye Weed
Eutrochium purpureum

AVERAGE DIMENSIONS
4-6' w x 5-8' h

FLOWER TIME:
July-September

This native species is tall, showy, fragrant, and beautiful. It requires moist soil that does not dry out. Prone to flopping.

Gateway Joe-Pye Weed
Eutrochium maculatum 'Gateway'

AVERAGE DIMENSIONS
36-48" w x 4-6' h

FLOWER TIME:
July-September

A shorter version of the native species that attracts pollinators.

Baby Joe-Pye Weed
Eutrochium dubium 'Baby Joe'

AVERAGE DIMENSIONS
24-36" w x 24-36" h

FLOWER TIME:
July-September

The shortest variety of Joe-Pye Weed makes it an excellent choice for many gardens.

Boneset
Eupatorium perfoliatum

SUN
 FULL SUN
 FILTERED SUN
 PART SHADE

SOIL
 MOIST SOIL
 FLUX SOIL
DRY SOIL

ATTRIBUTES
 POLLINATOR ATTRACTOR
FLOWERING PLANT
 LOW MAINTENANCE

AVERAGE DIMENSIONS
36-48" w x 36-48" h

FLOWER TIME:
July-September

DESCRIPTION:
This native perennial is found on the edges and margins of wetlands and stream banks and is well adapted for any shoreline garden. Boneset features large flat-topped clusters of white flowers that cover most of the plant and bloom for the latter part of the summer. This plant establishes quickly and requires little care. Pair Boneset with Joe-Pye Weed and Blazing Star for a stunning combination that will attract both people and butterflies.

Bottle Gentian
Gentiana andrewsii

SUN
 FULL SUN
 FILTERED SUN
 PART SHADE

SOIL
 MOIST SOIL
FLUX SOIL

ATTRIBUTES
 POLLINATOR ATTRACTOR
FLOWERING PLANT
 LOW MAINTENANCE

AVERAGE DIMENSIONS
6-12" w x 12-24" h

FLOWER TIME:
August-September

DESCRIPTION:
Bottle Gentian is a native wildflower that is found in moist woodlands and low areas near marshes and lakes. This plant is very unique and is almost never found in gardens. It is a slender perennial plant that pairs well with many plants, especially grasses. It's blue flowers form in closed clusters that never open. If left undisturbed and in optimal growing conditions in your garden, this plant will colonize into a larger clump. The Bottle Gentian does not like to be in dry soil or super hot conditions. Near the lake shore is the best place.

SUN   SOIL   ATTRIBUTES

FULL SUN   FILTERED SUN   PART SHADE   FULL SHADE   DRY SOIL   POLLINATOR ATTRACTOR   FALL COLOR   FLOWERING PLANT   LOW MAINTENANCE   BIRDS & WILDLIFE

Geranium
Geranium spp.

DESCRIPTION:

There are many Geranium species that we can grow in the garden. Many are familiar and widely used such as the Bloody Cranesbill Geranium. Many cultivars exist that form dense hummock that may spread depending on species and variety. Our native geranium, the Wild Geranium, is a great shade groundcover like flower (pictured middle). Geraniums are tough, adaptable and low maintenance. They do not, however, like wet feet.

AVERAGE DIMENSIONS
Variable depending on variety

FLOWER TIME:
June-August

Hosta
Hosta spp.

DESCRIPTION:

Hostas are an American garden standard. They are tough and dependable and thousands of varieties have been cultivated. Hostas are often a go-to plant for any shade garden. They have been used so prevalently that many gardeners have grown tired of them. Despite their popularity, Hostas have a place in any shade garden. Our favorite Hostas are the blue leaved varieties such as 'Halcyon' or 'Blue Angel'. Beware, Hostas are deer candy.

AVERAGE DIMENSIONS
Variable depending on variety

FLOWER TIME:
July-August

76

Daylily
Hemerocallis spp.

SUN

 FULL SUN FILTERED SUN PART SHADE

SOIL

 DRY SOIL

ATTRIBUTES

 POLLINATOR ATTRACTOR BIRDS & WILDLIFE FLOWERING PLANT EROSION CONTROL · LOW MAINTENANCE · TOUGH SOIL BUSTER

AVERAGE DIMENSIONS
Variable-depending on variety

FLOWER TIME:
June-October

DESCRIPTION:
Another American standard, the Daylily is a rugged, adaptable and vigorous perennial that will last in the garden many years or even decades. Daylilies are heavily used as a landscape plant because of their dependability. Every Daylily produces an abundance of flowers that will re-bloom for much of the season. Daylilies make a great plant for large extensive garden plantings that will be very low maintenance. This plant is also great for hillsides and areas that are to difficult to grow most plants.

Blue Flag Iris
Iris versicolor

SUN

 FULL SUN FILTERED SUN PART SHADE

SOIL

 WET SOIL MOIST SOIL · FLUX SOIL

ATTRIBUTES

 BIRDS & WILDLIFE · FLOWERING PLANT · LOW MAINTENANCE

AVERAGE DIMENSIONS
24-30" w x 24-36" h

FLOWER TIME:
May-June

DESCRIPTION:
Blue Flag Iris is the staple shoreline garden plant. In its native condition, it grows along lakes, wetlands, and streams. This Iris, native to Minnesota, is tough, long lasting, and blooms early in the year. Unlike many other Iris species, it maintains its attractive sword-like foliage throughout the season. The shoreline garden is the perfect setting for the Blue Flag Iris and is a logical start to your planting.

SUN
FULL SUN | FILTERED SUN

SOIL
MOIST SOIL | FLUX SOIL | DRY SOIL

ATTRIBUTES
POLLINATOR ATTRACTOR | BIRDS & WILDLIFE | FLOWERING PLANT | WINTER INTEREST | LOW MAINTENANCE | TOUGH SOIL BUSTER

Blazing Star
Liatris spicata 'Kobold'

DESCRIPTION:
The Blazing Star is a brilliant and striking mid to late summer bloomer. Its vertical spike of vibrant purple flowers punctuate the garden planting. The 'Kobold' Blazing Star is an excellent cultivar because of its compact habit and dense floral dislplay. Pairs well with Coneflower, Black Eyed Susan, Milkweed and Sedum.

AVERAGE DIMENSIONS
12-18" w x 18-30" h

FLOWER TIME:
July-August

SUN
FULL SUN | FILTERED SUN

SOIL
DRY SOIL

ATTRIBUTES
POLLINATOR ATTRACTOR | FLOWERING PLANT | LOW MAINTENANCE

Sea Lavender
Limonium platyphyllum

DESCRIPTION:
Sea Lavender is a low mounding plant that has an airy appearance. It commonly grows in dry and sometimes even salty conditions. It is drought tolerant and should not be placed in wet conditions near the shoreline edge. Sea lavender is an excellent plant for cut flowers. It is also highly attractive to butterflies and pollinators. It pairs well with Blazing Star, Butterfly Milkweed, and Purple Coneflower.

AVERAGE DIMENSIONS
24-30" w x 24-30" h

FLOWER TIME:
June-August

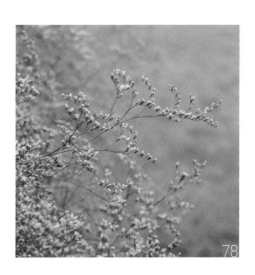

78

Bee Balm
Monarda spp.

SUN
 FULL SUN
 FILTERED SUN

SOIL
 DRY SOIL

ATTRIBUTES
 POLLINATOR ATTRACTOR
 BIRDS & WILDLIFE
 FLOWERING PLANT
LOW MAINTENANCE

DESCRIPTION:

Bee Balm is one of the showiest summer-blooming perennials. Wild Bergamot, the native species, is usually found in hillsides, meadows and prairies. Its unique spotted purple flower is a show stopper. Monarda can also provide excellent winter and late fall interest. Several varieties have been cultivated for new flower colors, such as blue-purple, deep red, and pink. The boldness of Monarda makes it well suited for massing. Monarda prefers the drier, well-drained soils away from the moisture of lake's edge. It pairs well with Purple Coneflower, Daylilies, and Beardstongue.

Wild Bergamot
Monarda fistulosa

AVERAGE DIMENSIONS
24-30" w x 24-48" h

FLOWER TIME:
June-September

The most popular and wide spread species of Monarda. The pink/purple flowers resemble frayed pom poms. Susceptible to powdery mildew.

Bradbury's Monarda
Mondarda bradburiana

AVERAGE DIMENSIONS
18-30" w x 24-30" h

FLOWER TIME:
June-September

This unique species is seldom used, but is a mid-summer flower. A shorter plant with a lighter, spotted flower.

Many varieties of Bee Balm have been cultivated with different sizes and flower colors. 'Blue Stocking', 'Raspberry Wine', and 'Jacob Cline' are just a few of the many available.

SUN

FULL SUN · FILTERED SUN · PART SHADE

SOIL

DRY SOIL

ATTRIBUTES

POLLINATOR ATTRACTOR · FLOWERING PLANT · LOW MAINTENANCE · TOUGH SOIL BUSTER

Catmint
Nepeta spp.

DESCRIPTION:

Catmint is a very useful garden plant. It forms a dense and low mound of foliage that blooms nearly all season long beginning in May. It has a profuse display of deep purple flowers. During full bloom in the early Summer, Catmint is often covered with pollinators and beneficial insects. Catmint makes an excellent edge to a perennial border and can be used in nearly any garden. It is easy to grow and maintain and fits in both formal and more naturalistic plantings.

AVERAGE DIMENSIONS
36-48" w x 18-30" h

FLOWER TIME:
May-September

SUN

FULL SUN · FILTERED SUN

SOIL

DRY SOIL

ATTRIBUTES

POLLINATOR ATTRACTOR · BIRDS & WILDLIFE · FLOWERING PLANT · LOW MAINTENANCE

Beardstongue
Penstemon 'Husker Red'

DESCRIPTION:

Beardstongue, in particular, the Husker Red Beardstongue is a wonderful perennial. It's early flush of pink-white tubular blooms are an early season treat. It's reddish foliage helps break up the greens that often dominate the perennial garden in June. Beardstongue does not like wet feet so be careful not to plant too close to the shoreline.

AVERAGE DIMENSIONS
12-24" w x 24-36" h

FLOWER TIME:
May-June

Russian Sage
Perovskia atriplicifolia

SUN
 FULL SUN
 FILTERED SUN

SOIL
 DRY SOIL

ATTRIBUTES
  POLLINATOR ATTRACTOR
FLOWERING PLANT
 LOW MAINTENANCE
 TOUGH SOIL BUSTER

AVERAGE DIMENSIONS
24-30" w x 24-48" h

FLOWER TIME:
June-September

DESCRIPTION:
Russian Sage is woody-base perennial of the mint family. It will often grow to four feet high with the top two feet covered with fine purple flowers that are wonderfully aromatic. This plant requires dry conditions. Russian Sage works well as a back drop within a perennial garden. It pairs well with Purple Coneflower, Black Eyed Susan, and taller ornamental grasses.

Obedient Plant
Physostegia virginiana

SUN
 FULL SUN
 FILTERED SUN

SOIL
 MOIST SOIL
 FLUX SOIL
 DRY SOIL

ATTRIBUTES
 POLLINATOR ATTRACTOR
 BIRDS & WILDLIFE
FLOWERING PLANT

AVERAGE DIMENSIONS
24-36" w x 30-48" h

FLOWER TIME:
June-September

DESCRIPTION:
Obedient Plant is a vigorous and spreading perennial that is useful in wet conditions where weed competition is high. It gets its name "Obedient" because you can push its flowers into new positions and it will stay. However, it is not very obedient about staying in one place, spreading and re-seeding prolifically. In its native condition, it is often found in wet prairies, stream banks and other wet locations. This plant is best used in more naturalistic plantings where it can be allowed to spread.

SUN
 FULL SUN
 FILTERED SUN
 PART SHADE

SOIL
 DRY SOIL

ATTRIBUTES
 POLLINATOR ATTRACTOR
 FLOWERING PLANT
 LOW MAINTENANCE

Blunt Mountain Mint
Pycnanthemum muticum

DESCRIPTION:

Blunt Mountain Mint is a clump forming and aromatic perennial that is not well known or widely used in gardens and landscapes. This plant has a full form, sweet smell and attracts countless pollinators. In fact, this plant is considered the number one plant for pollinators at the world famous Lurie Garden in Chicago, IL. Blunt Mountain Mint pairs well with Arkansas Blue Star, Blazing Stars and many grasses.

AVERAGE DIMENSIONS
24-36" w x 24-36" h

FLOWER TIME:
July-September

SUN
 FULL SUN
 FILTERED SUN

SOIL
 FLUX SOIL
 DRY SOIL

ATTRIBUTES
 POLLINATOR ATTRACTOR
 FLOWERING PLANT
 LOW MAINTENANCE
 TOUGH SOIL BUSTER
 BIRDS & WILDLIFE

Black Eyed Susan
Rudbeckia fulgida 'Goldsturm'

DESCRIPTION:

Black Eyed Susan is another tried and true perennial. The Goldsturm variety won the 1999 Perennial Plant Association's Plant of the Year award. Its large, coarse leaves form a dense mound with upright flower stems protruding to form a bold display of golden yellow blooms. This plant will attract many pollinators and birds will eat the seeds during the winter. Pairs well with Purple Coneflower, Blazing Stars and Russian Sage.

AVERAGE DIMENSIONS
18-24" w x 24-30" h

FLOWER TIME:
June-September

Meadow Sage
Salvia spp.

SUN
 FULL SUN
 FILTERED SUN

SOIL
 DRY SOIL

ATTRIBUTES
 POLLINATOR ATTRACTOR
FLOWERING PLANT
 LOW MAINTENANCE
 BIRDS & WILDLIFE

AVERAGE DIMENSIONS
12-24" w x 12-24" h

FLOWER TIME:
May-June

DESCRIPTION:
Meadow Sage or Salvia is very common garden plant that features bold, upright purple flowers that bring life to the early summer garden. Many varieties are widely available that give you several options of size and color. Try to mix 3 to 4 different varieties in a large mass to create a naturalistic meadow effect (bottom right). Salvia makes an excellent cut flower, plus this flower will re-bloom if dead headed in mid summer.

Sedum
Sedum telephinum 'Autumn Joy'

SUN
 FULL SUN
 FILTERED SUN
 PART SHADE

SOIL
DRY SOIL

ATTRIBUTES
 POLLINATOR ATTRACTOR
FLOWERING PLANT
 WINTER INTEREST
 LOW MAINTENANCE

AVERAGE DIMENSIONS
24-30" w x 24-36" h

FLOWER TIME:
June-September

DESCRIPTION:
The Autumn Joy Sedum is nearly as dependable and tough as they come. It is a drought tolerant succulent that never requires any irrigation and its bold umbels of flowers will attract countless pollinators. This plant has all season interest. It is one of the first plants to start growing in the spring and it often has a beautiful winter form. It pairs well with Blazing Star, Purple Coneflower and Salvia. This Sedum prefers well-drained conditions and should not be placed too near the wet area of the shoreline.

FULL SUN · FILTERED SUN · PART SHADE · MOIST SOIL · FLUX SOIL · DRY SOIL · POLLINATOR ATTRACTOR · FLOWERING PLANT · LOW MAINTENANCE · TOUGH SOIL BUSTER

Fireworks Goldenrod
Solidago rugosa 'Fireworks'

DESCRIPTION:
Fireworks Goldenrod is an exciting new introduction that has many of the same habitat benefits of the native goldenrods, but with far more reliability and tameness, making it far better suited for the garden. The flower of the Fireworks Goldenrod forms a beautiful cascade of yellow that resembles a bursting firework. This plant will attract many pollinators and has a very wild appearance.

AVERAGE DIMENSIONS
24-36" w x 36-48" h

FLOWER TIME:
September-October

SUN | SOIL | ATTRIBUTES

FULL SUN · FILTERED SUN · PART SHADE · MOIST SOIL · FLUX SOIL · DRY SOIL · POLLINATOR ATTRACTOR · FLOWERING PLANT · LOW MAINTENANCE

Golden Alexanders
Zizia aurea

DESCRIPTION:
Golden Alexanders is often found in colonies growing in moist woods, thickets, glades and prairies. It has foliage near the base of the plant with upright stems that feature umbels of yellow flowers that bloom in early spring. Golden Alexanders will often seed around so it might be best suited in more wild or naturalistic style gardens.

AVERAGE DIMENSIONS
24-48" w x 24-30" h

FLOWER TIME:
May-June

84

Sideoats Grama
Bouteloua curtipendula

SUN
FULL SUN

SOIL
DRY SOIL

ATTRIBUTES
FALL COLOR   EROSION CONTROL   LOW MAINTENANCE   TOUGH SOIL BUSTER

AVERAGE DIMENSIONS
18-30" w x 18-30" h

DESCRIPTION:
Sideoats Grama is an interesting native grass that is seldom used in gardens. Typically found growing in rocky outcrops and mixed grass prairies, Sideoats Grama is well suited to dry soils and projects where drought tolerance is paramount. Its unique seedhead resembling oats hanging sideways from the stem, is perhaps its most desirable trait. The fall season brings a striking golden color that turns to bronze.

Blonde Ambition Grama
Bouteloua gracilis 'Blonde Ambition'

SUN
FULL SUN   FILTERED SUN

SOIL
DRY SOIL

ATTRIBUTES
FALL COLOR   LOW MAINTENANCE   TOUGH SOIL BUSTER

AVERAGE DIMENSIONS
24-30" w x 24-36" h

CULTIVARS:
'Blonde Ambition'

DESCRIPTION:
This unusual ornamental grass is sure to excite any gardener. Its eyelash-like seedhead forms in mid-summer and will often last well into the winter. Adapted from a native short grass, this clumping grass is graceful and sophisticated in its appearance. It is extremely cold hardy and adaptable to many soil types as long as they are well drained. Use Blonde Ambition in large masses and sweeps to create drama and movement. Pairs well with Little Bluestem, Catmint, Autumn Joy Sedum, and Salvia.

SUN			SOIL		ATTRIBUTES		

FULL SUN	FILTERED SUN	PART SHADE	FLUX SOIL	DRY SOIL	WINTER INTEREST	LOW MAINTENANCE	TOUGH SOIL BUSTER

Karl Foerster Grass
Calamagrostis x acutiflora 'Karl Foerster'

DESCRIPTION:

Karl Foerster Feather Reed Grass is one of the most popular ornamental grasses available. Its dependability and adaptability make it a logical addition to any garden. Its stiff and upright habit stands tall in the garden. Its golden seedhead emerges mid summer and complements many flowering perennials. Karl Foerster Grass is also one of the few ornamental grasses that can tolerate some shade. This grass is well suited for many soil types, but prefers a moist, well-drained condition.

AVERAGE DIMENSIONS
24-36" w x 48-54" h

CULTIVARS:
'Karl Foerster'
'Avalanche'
'Overdam'

SUN			SOIL		ATTRIBUTES		

FULL SUN	FILTERED SUN	PART SHADE	FLUX SOIL	DRY SOIL	FALL COLOR	LOW MAINTENANCE	TOUGH SOIL BUSTER

Korean Feather Grass
Calamagrostis brachytricha

DESCRIPTION:

Korean Feather Grass is an interesting and fall-blooming alternative to the popular Karl Foerster Grass. Korean Feather Grass is clump-forming, dependable and produces an airy, pinkish flower plume that catches the fall sunlight. It is tolerant of a wide range of soil types from sandy to clay and can tolerate a fair amount of shade. This warm season grass may not have much to show early in the season, but its dramatic fall display is well worth it. Pairs well with Bee Balm, Blunt Mountain Mint, Sedum, and Coneflower.

AVERAGE DIMENSIONS
24-30" w x 36-48" h

86

Sedge
Carex spp.

SUN

FULL SUN | PART SHADE | FULL SHADE

SOIL

WET SOIL | MOIST SOIL | FLUX SOIL | DRY SOIL

ATTRIBUTES

EROSION CONTROL | LOW MAINTENANCE

DESCRIPTION:

The Sedges are a unique genus of plants that are grass-like in appearance, but not actually grasses. Typically evergreen, Sedges are used ornamentally for their foliage and fine textures. Nearly 500 of species exist in North America, but only a handful are available in the nursery. Sedges can be used as accent specimens as mass plantings or as groundcovers. Some Sedge species prefer very wet conditions and others prefer dry conditions.

Pennsylvania Sedge
Carex pennsylvanica

AVERAGE DIMENSIONS
8-12" w x 6-9" h

FLOWER TIME:
March-April

An excellent, shade tolerant groundcover with very fine texture. This Sedge can be used full sun or full shade in dry conditions.

Fox Sedge
Carex vulpinoidea

AVERAGE DIMENSIONS
18-24" w x 24-36" h

FLOWER TIME:
June-September

This larger Sedge prefers moist and wet conditions. The seedheads that emerge in late summer resemble fox tails.

Tussock Sedge
Carex stricta

AVERAGE DIMENSIONS
24-30" w x 24-36" h

FLOWER TIME:
June-September

A wetland native that forms dense bunches of foliage. It prefers very wet conditions, but can tolerate slightly drier spots as well.

SUN

FULL
SUN

FILTERED
SUN

PART
SHADE

SOIL

FLUX
SOIL

DRY
SOIL

ATTRIBUTES

BIRDS &
WILDLIFE

LOW
MAINTENANCE

Tufted Hair Grass
Deschampsia cespitosa

DESCRIPTION:

Tufted Hair Grass is a tough and resilient clump-forming grass that produces an airy mass of seed heads above a rounded tuft of dark green blades. This cool season grass greens up early in the spring and produces its showy seedhead mid-summer. It prefers well drained conditions, but can tolerate extended moisture and even some shade. Plant this grass in large masses to produce a ghostly effect in the fall. Pairs well with Anise Hyssop, Blazing Star, Sedum, and Salvia.

AVERAGE DIMENSIONS
12-24" w x 24-36" h

CULTIVARS:
'Schottland'
'Northern Lights'
'Goldehange'

SUN

FILTERED
SUN

PART
SHADE

FULL
SHADE

SOIL

DRY
SOIL

ATTRIBUTES

FALL
COLOR

LOW
MAINTENANCE

Japanese Forest Grass
Hakonechloa macra 'Aureola'

DESCRIPTION:

Native to mountainous areas of Japan, Japanese Forest Grass is the go-to ornamental grass for shady areas. Its golden foliage illuminates the dark greens of the shade garden. Forming a dense clump of slender leaves, Japanese Forest Grass has a graceful and elegant appearance. Its leaves resemble bamboo and can give a unique feel to your garden. It prefers moist, shady conditions, but can tolerate full sun if the soil stays evenly moist.

AVERAGE DIMENSIONS
24-30" w x 18-24" h

CULTIVARS:
'Aureola'
'All Gold'

Soft Rush
Juncus effusus

SUN
FULL SUN · FILTERED SUN

SOIL
WET SOIL · MOIST SOIL · FLUX SOIL · DRY SOIL

ATTRIBUTES
BIRDS & WILDLIFE · FLOWERING PLANT · WINTER INTEREST · LOW MAINTENANCE

AVERAGE DIMENSIONS
12-24" w x 24-36" h

DESCRIPTION:
Soft Rush is a clump forming wetland plant that offers a vertical accent to your shoreline garden. Often found on the edge of wetlands, Soft Rush prefers a moist soil but can tolerate average garden conditions. The straight and spike like leaves of this plant make a striking effect. A small golden flower that turns brown throughout the season emerges from each spike.

Switchgrass
Panicum virgatum

SUN
FULL SUN · FILTERED SUN

SOIL
FLUX SOIL · DRY SOIL

ATTRIBUTES
FALL COLOR · BIRDS & WILDLIFE · WINTER INTEREST · EROSION CONTROL · LOW MAINTENANCE · TOUGH SOIL BUSTER

AVERAGE DIMENSIONS
24-30" w x 24-36" h

CULTIVARS:
'Shenandoah'
'Heavy Metal'
'Dewey Blues'
'Prairie Fire'

DESCRIPTION:
Switchgrass is a robust and tall native grass. It can tolerate a very wide range of soil types and is very difficult to kill. The native strain can be quite aggressive. It is recommend to use one of the many cultivated varieties which feature unique foliage and seedheads. Switchgrass can be used to provide a naturalistic effect in the garden, as specimen accent, or as a low maintenance massing. The airy seedhead catches the wind and gives life to the garden.

Little Bluestem
Schizachyrium scoparium

DESCRIPTION:
Little Bluestem is perhaps the most widely used native grass in gardens and built landscapes. Its bright fall color and drought tolerance make it a popular choice. Native to prairies and dunes across North America, Little Bluestem is a tough plant capable of developing a very deep root system. Native strains can potentially be floppy or seed prolificly. Several cultivated varieties have been developed for more showy fall color and more compact habits.

AVERAGE DIMENSIONS
24-30" w x 24-36" h

CULTIVARS:
Blue Heaven®
'Blaze'
'The Blues'

SUN | SOIL | ATTRIBUTES

FULL SUN | FILTERED SUN | DRY SOIL | FALL COLOR | LOW MAINTENANCE

Autumn Moor Grass
Sesleria autumnalis

AVERAGE DIMENSIONS
18-24" w x 18-24" h

DESCRIPTION:
Autumn Moor Grass is a small, upright, clump-forming grass that begins growing early in the spring with bright chartreuse foliage. Long, silvery-brown seedheads develop late in the summer. Seldom used, this grass will add a unique flavor to your garden. Plant Autumn Moor Grass in large massings as a groundcover, on slopes, or under the light shade of trees. Native to Southern Europe, this grass is non-invasive and performs well in many situations. Pair with purple flowering perennials such as Salvia, Catmint, or Anise Hyssop for a vibrant contrast.

Prairie Dropseed
Sporobolus heterolepis

SUN
 FULL SUN
 FILTERED SUN

SOIL
 DRY SOIL

ATTRIBUTES
 FALL COLOR
 BIRDS & WILDLIFE
 LOW MAINTENANCE
TOUGH SOIL BUSTER

AVERAGE DIMENSIONS
24-30" w x 24-36" h

FLOWER TIME:
June-September

DESCRIPTION:

Prairie Dropseed is a long-lived ornamental grass that forms a full clump of fine textured blades. Its gallant appearance makes it suitable for nearly any style of garden. In the late summer, Prairie Dropseed produces open and airy seedheads that shine in the light or produce backdrop for flowering perennials such as Sedum, Coneflower, Blazing Star or Salvia. Prairie Dropseed can also be used as a large scale groundcover or turf replacement.

Low Mow Lawn
Festuca spp., Buchloe dactyloides

SUN
 FULL SUN
FILTERED SUN
 PART SHADE

SOIL
 DRY SOIL

ATTRIBUTES
 LOW MAINTENANCE

DESCRIPTION:

Traditional turfgrass can be replaced with low mow varieties. Properly installed, these planting methods can look great and be much lower maintenance than conventional turfgrass. For instance, low-mow grass varieties only need to be mowed every 4-6 weeks. Low-mow turfgrasses are developed as a blend of various grass species designed to be very low input (fertilizer, irrigation, labor) while still creating a lush green carpet of grass. How often you decide to mow it will determine how it looks. Mow it frequently (every 1-2 weeks) and it will resemble a traditional lawn. Mow it every 4-6 weeks and it will have a much more shaggy appearance.

BOWIE BUFFALO GRASS

LOW MOW FESCUE

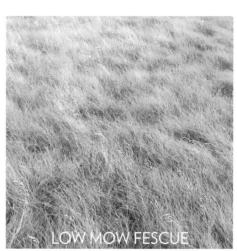
LOW MOW FESCUE

SUN
 FULL SUN
 FILTERED SUN
 PART SHADE

SOIL
 MOIST SOIL
FLUX SOIL
DRY SOIL

ATTRIBUTES
 FALL COLOR
 BIRDS & WILDLIFE
FLOWERING PLANT
LOW MAINTENANCE

Black Chokeberry
Aronia melanocarpa

DESCRIPTION:
Black Chokeberry is a tall, vase-shaped shrub that is truly an all season plant. The spring brings an array of fragrant white flowers, followed by the production of dark glossy leaves and deep purple fruits. The fall brings a brilliant show of orange-red leaves. Native to Minnesota, this shrub provides a fruit source for many bird species. Many cultivated varieties are available, providing options for smaller sizes and more compact forms.

AVERAGE DIMENSIONS
3-6' w x 3-6' h

FLOWER TIME:
April-May

SUGGESTED VARIETY:
'Autumn Magic'

SUN
 FULL SUN
 FILTERED SUN
 PART SHADE

SOIL
 MOIST SOIL
FLUX SOIL
DRY SOIL

ATTRIBUTES
 POLLINATOR ATTRACTOR
BIRDS & WILDLIFE
FLOWERING PLANT
LOW MAINTENANCE

Clethra
Clethra alnifolia

DESCRIPTION:
Clethra or Summersweet is an upright to rounded shrub that can reach 4-6' in height depending on variety. Best known for its intensely fragrant flowers, Clethra produces white spike blooms in mid summer that will attract people and butterflies alike. Clethra is tolerant of a fair amount of shade and moist soils. Plant in full sun and evenly moist soil for maximum flowering. Even outside of flowering, the rounded habit makes for an attractive and handsome shrub.

AVERAGE DIMENSIONS
3-5' w x 3-5' h

FLOWER TIME:
July

SUGGESTED VARIETY:
'Hummingbird'

Dogwood
Cornus spp.

SUN
 FULL SUN
 FILTERED SUN
 PART SHADE

SOIL
 WET SOIL
 MOIST SOIL
 FLUX SOIL
 DRY SOIL

ATTRIBUTES
 FALL COLOR
 BIRDS & WILDLIFE
 FLOWERING PLANT
 WINTER INTEREST
 EROSION CONTROL
LOW MAINTENANCE
TOUGH SOIL BUSTER

AVERAGE DIMENSIONS
24-30" w x 24-36" h

FLOWER TIME:
Late May-June

DESCRIPTION:
Dogwood is a popular genus of shrub that are commonly used in landscapes and gardens for their dependability and dramatic winter interest. Several species are native to the wetland edges and swamps of Minnesota, but nearly all native species grow to very large sizes (~12-15') which may not be well suited for most gardens. However, many smaller cultivated varieties exist that retain the resilient qualities of the native variety and are well suited for any shoreline garden.

Arctic Fire Dogwood
Cornus stolonifera 'Farrow'

AVERAGE DIMENSIONS
3-4' w x 3-4' h

NOTES:
A compact shrub with a rounded habit. Leaves turn a deep burgundy color in the fall. Deep scarlet red branches for winter interest.

Red Gnome Dogwood
Cornus alba siberica 'Regnzam'

AVERAGE DIMENSIONS
3-4' w x 3-4' h

NOTES:
A compact, low-growing shrub with a rounded habit. Pointed leaves are tinged with red tips and turn a dull purple in the fall. Winter stems are profusely red.

Isanti Dogwood
Cornus sericea 'Isanti'

AVERAGE DIMENSIONS
5-7' w x 4-6' h

A slower growing dogwood that is very close to the native variety, but only reaches 6' in height. Provides excellent habitat for birds.

AVERAGE DIM[ENSIONS]
30-42" w x 24-[36" h]

FLOWER TIME:
May-June

DESCRIPTION:

A tough and relatively small shrub that is best used in large masses and hard to plant areas. Tolerant of a wide variety of conditions and able to thrive with little care, this plant is nearly a no maintenance plant. Foliage is bronze-green turning a deep red in the fall. Small yellow flowers bloom in late spring and early summer. Plant in large masses to replace lawn or use in wooded areas to compete with buckthorn and garlic mustard.

AVERAGE DIMENSIONS
3-6' w x 3-6' h

FLOWER TIME:
June-September

DESCRIPTION:

Hydrangeas are a commonly used landscape plant that have a place in the shoreline garden. They produce large, vibrant blooms and are often very easy to grow. Several species and cultivated varieties exist that give you a wide range of sizes, flower types and colors. The standard Annabelle Hydrangea has large white ball-like flowers, while the species paniculata presents several varieties such as 'Pinky Winky' or 'Limelight' have a cone shape flower ranging in color from pink to white to lime green.

SUN

| FULL SUN | FILTERED SUN | PART SHADE |

SOIL

| WET SOIL | MOIST SOIL | FLUX SOIL |

ATTRIBUTES

| BIRDS & WILDLIFE | WINTER INTEREST | LOW MAINTENANCE |

DESCRIPTION:

...terberry is a slow growing deciduous shrub that is often found along stream banks ...lake edges making it a great addition to your shoreline garden. Best known for its ...ht red berries that persist throughout the winter, Winterberry can bring life to your ...ter garden and thrive in very wet conditions during the growing season. Winterberry is a dioecious plant, which means that each plant is either male or female. A planting requires both males and females present to produce berries on the female shrubs.

Ninebark
Physocarpus opulifolius

SUN

| FULL SUN | FILTERED SUN | PART SHADE |

SOIL

| DRY SOIL |

ATTRIBUTES

| POLLINATOR ATTRACTOR | FLOWERING PLANT | LOW MAINTENANCE |

AVERAGE DIMENSIONS
3-6' w x 3-6' h

FLOWER TIME:
June

SUGGESTED VARIETY:
'Summer Wine'
'Donna May'

DESCRIPTION:

Ninebark is a mound-shaped shrub with arching branches and exfoliating bark. The native species is found on dry bluffs, hillsides, and thickets. It has green leaves and often grows to nearly 12 feet tall. Several cultivated varieties have been developed that are smaller in size (4-6') and with burgundy colored foliage. The deep foliage makes this plant an effective specimen or accent that helps break up the green in the garden. Be sure to place Ninebark in dry locations as it prefers dry soil and has potential to develop powdery mildew.

95

SUN

FULL SUN

FILTERED SUN

SOIL

DRY SOIL

ATTRIBUTES

FALL COLOR

BIRDS & WILDLIFE

EROSION CONTROL

LOW MAINTENANCE

TOUGH SOIL BUSTER

DESCRIPTION:

Sumac are extremely resilient and drought tolerant shrubs that often grow in tough and disturbed areas s
as hillsides, roadsides, and banks. Smooth and Staghorn Sumac are often seen growing as small colonie
along highways and freeways. Its deep red fall foliage is stunning and provides a moment of true drama.
Sumac provide food and cover for many species of bird as well. This workhorse of a plant can be aggressive
and is best used for large-scale turf replacement or steep slope stabilizations. Mature sumac colonies can
be cut back to keep the overall height shorter and more even in appearance.

Gro-Low Sumac

Rhus aromatica 'Gro-Low'

AVERAGE DIMENSIONS
4-6' w x 2-3' h

A low-growing, wide spreading selection of fragrant sumac with excellent orange-red fall color. Looks disimiliar from other sumacs. Great for mass plantings or erosion control. Also very drought and salt tolerant.

Smooth Sumac

Rhus glabra

AVERAGE DIMENSIONS
spreading w x 6-10' h

A wide spreading and suckering shrub with smooth bark that also has beautiful fall foliage. Excellent for erosion control on steep banks and hillsides.

Staghorn Sumac

Rhus typhina

AVERAGE DIMENSIONS
20-30' w x 15-25' h

Another colonizing shrub with dramatic red fall tones. Staghorn sumac grows much taller. If grown as a specimen it resembles more of a tree. In winter, the bare twisting stems resemble deer antlers.

SUN			SOIL		ATTRIBUTES			
FULL SUN	FILTERED SUN	PART SHADE	FLUX SOIL	DRY SOIL	BIRDS & WILDLIFE	WINTER INTEREST	LOW MAINTENANCE	TOUGH SOIL BUSTER

Sumac
Rhus spp.

'Techny'
'Holmstrup'

CRIPTION:

White Cedar or Arborvitae, as it is more commonly known, is a tough evergreen that is often used as a specimen or a hedge. Native to most of the Eastern U.S. and ada, the tree form White Cedar often grows to 40' or 50' in cool, moist areas near water bodies. Recent horticultural cultivation has developed many new varities that are shorter and grown in differing forms such as pyramidal and globe. Arborvitae can be used very effectively as a hedge to create formal edge and structure in your garden.

Highbush Blueberry
Vaccinium corymbosum

SUN			SOIL			ATTRIBUTES			
FULL SUN	FILTERED SUN	PART SHADE	MOIST SOIL	FLUX SOIL	DRY SOIL	FALL COLOR	BIRDS & WILDLIFE	FLOWERING PLANT	LOW MAINTENANCE

AVERAGE DIMENSIONS
6-10' w x 6-10' h

FLOWER TIME:
June

DESCRIPTION:

Highbush Blueberry is an upright, deciduous shrub that prefers slightly wet locations, but can also tolerate dry conditions. This adaptability makes it a useful plant for shoreline gardens, especially those with a more naturalized aesthetic. Small, tubular, white flowers develop in mid summer and edible fruits show up in late summer. If you don't eat the berries, the birds will. Fall foliage is often bright red and dramatic.

SUN

FULL SUN | FILTERED SUN | PART SHADE | FULL SHADE

SOIL

FLUX SOIL | DRY SOIL

ATTRIBUTES

FALL COLOR | BIRDS & WILDLIFE | FLOWERING PLANT | LOW MAINTENANCE | TOUGH SOIL BUSTER

Viburnum
Viburnum spp.

DESCRIPTION:

The Viburnums are a genus of native shrubs that are most commonly found on woodland edges and thickets. These medium sized shrubs often have showy flowers, large groupings of fruits and attractive fall foliage. Viburnums are also quite shade tolerant making them a useful plant under trees and for screening. Many species of birds are attracted to Viburnums for their fruit. There are many cultivated varieties that have a smaller size and more even growth habit.

Arrowwood Viburnum
Viburnum dentatum

AVERAGE DIMENSIONS
10-12' w x 10-12' h

An upright shrub with straight, erect stems that were used for arrow shafts by indigenous peoples. Cultivated varieties such as Blue Muffin®, Mohican, or Northern Burgundy® are excellent selections

Highbush Cranberry
Viburnum trilobum

AVERAGE DIMENSIONS
5-6' w x 5-6' h

Rounded form shrub with white flowers and red fruits. Partial branch dieback is common. 'Bailey Compact' and 'Wentworth' are great varieties with tighter form and habit.

Nannyberry
Viburnum lentago

AVERAGE DIMENSIONS
15-20' w x 8-15' h

A tall shrub, often growing as a tree. Slender, arching branches provide an open, loose habit. Provides a critical food source for many birds. Very wild in its aesthetic, it is perfect for naturalized woodland edges.

PHOTO CREDITS

All photographs by Michael Keenan unless otherwise noted. Credits listed from left to right, top to bottom, unless otherwise noted.

CPSIA information can be obtained at www.ICGtesting.com
Printed in the USA
BVIW12n0103270218
509201BV00006B/30